CHALLENGE 2000

The Race to Win the America's Cup

CHALLENGE 2000
The Race to Win the *America's Cup*

By Russell Coutts and Paul Larsen

With photography by
Daniel Forster and Dan Nerney

TIME LIFE BOOKS

ALEXANDRIA, VIRGINIA

TIME-LIFE BOOKS IS A DIVISION OF TIME LIFE INC.

TIME LIFE INC.
President and CEO: George Artandi

TIME-LIFE CUSTOM PUBLISHING
Vice President and Publisher   Terry Newell
Vice President of Sales and Marketing   Neil Levin
Director of Acquisitions and Editorial Resources   Jennifer Pearce
Director of Creative Services   Laura Ciccone McNeill
Director of Special Markets   Liz Ziehl
Project Manager   Jennie Halfant
Technical Specialist   Monika Lynde
Director of Quality Assurance   James D. King
Production Manager   Carolyn Bounds

Printed in England.
10 9 8 7 6 5 4 3 2 1
TIME-LIFE is a trademark of Time Warner Inc., and affiliated companies.

Library of Congress Cataloging-in-Publication Data
Coutts, Russell
        Challenge 2000 : the race to win the America's Cup / Russell Coutts and Paul Larsen.
            p.   cm.
        Includes index.
        ISBN 0-7370-0059-7   (hc.)
        1. America's Cup 2. America's Cup Pictorial works. I. Larsen Paul C,. 1947–   . II. Title
    GV 829.C693   1999   99-41410
        797.1'4—dc21   CIP

Books produced by Time-Life Custom Publishing are available at a special bulk discount for promotional and premium
use. Custom adaptations can also be created to meet your specific marketing goals. Call 1-800-323-5255.

CONTENTS

The 100 Guineas Cup / 8

From Plastic to Silver / 40

A Perfect Venue / 58

America's Cup Technology / 70

Racing One on One / 88

For the Defense: Team New Zealand / 112

The Challengers / 124

Appendix / 186

Index / 188

Photo Credits / 192

ACKNOWLEDGMENTS

The authors give special thanks and sincere appreciation to Carlton J. Pinheiro, Curator of the Herreshoff Marine Museum and the America's Cup Hall of Fame. Mr. Pinheiro made an exhaustive search of the Museum's archives to locate many rare photographs, some never before published, to help illustrate the history of this unique sporting event.

Photographer Paul Darling also deserves special mention for his contribution of images of the early 12-meter races, including what is believed to be the first color photograph ever taken of America's Cup action. And the photographic record included in this book would not have been possible without the work of Daniel Forster and Dan Nerney.

We also owe a large debt to the many America's Cup writers and historians who came before us, especially:
John Rousmaniere, Stanley Rosenfeld, Roger Vaughan, John Bertrand, Bob Fisher, Michael Levitt, Barbara Lloyd, Thomas Lawson, Winfield M. Thompson, Dennis Conner, Bob Bavier, Bruce Stannard, Ivor Wilkens, and Doug Riggs.

Jennie Halfant at Time Life kept a steady hand on the helm throughout the voyage from manuscript to finished book. Thanks for the help.

Many other friends and colleagues assisted in numerous ways, including: Scott MacLeod, Gay Larsen, Peter Scott, Kristen Sneyd, Jamie France, Nick Holroyd, Sarah Beresford, Janette Howe, Tom Schnackenberg, and D. J. Cathcart.

Russell Coutts
Paul Larsen
August 25, 1999

The 100 Guineas Cup

THE CELEBRATED YACHT "AMERICA".

WINNER OF THE "QUEEN'S CUP," VALUE 100 GUINEAS.

In the Royal Yacht Squadron Match for all Nations at Cowes, England, Aug. 22. 1851.

CHAPTER ONE

THE 100 GUINEAS CUP

What is it about the America's Cup that has motivated the thousands of sailors, designers, technicians, and syndicate heads who have aspired to win it for 148 years? Other than the 134 ounces of sterling silver that constitute the 27-inch-high trophy, there is no fortune awarded. Instead, personal sacrifice in the form of separation from family, friends, and finances has customarily marked the quest. For the winners, fame has been elusive. Controversy, contention, and conflict have more often been the results of victory.

It is often said that attempting to win the oldest trophy

America—pictured in the handsome Currier and Ives lithograph at left—wrested the so-called 100 Guineas Cup from a fleet of 15 British yachts in 1851. The race was then auspiciously renamed the America's Cup and a 132-year American winning streak in New York Harbor and Newport, Rhode Island, was begun.

in international competition is the biggest gamble in all of sport. Considering the vast sums of money invested in the effort—anywhere from an estimated $15 million to $50 million per team for the 1999/2000 event—it is hard to identify another contest in which so much is at stake for so little real monetary return.

The lure of a big money payoff is present, of course, but not in the traditional sense. The victorious team wins the right to hold the next event at a venue of its choosing, and the host city can profit handsomely. The losing teams return home and attempt to square things with their supporters.

Other than glory, personal satisfaction, potential product endorsements, and a name inscribed on the trophy, the spoils of victory are ephemeral at best. Some sailors and designers will realize a boost in reputation that can be leveraged for increased fees. Others will

This rare photograph of the famous yacht designer Nathanael Herreshoff (left), also known as the "Wizard of Bristol," was taken in 1920. Vigilant *(right) was the first of a record six Herreshoff designs to successfully defend the America's Cup. It was 124 feet in length, rigged as a sloop and required a crew of 70. The Wizard himself was the victorious helmsman in three races against* Valkyrie II *in 1893.*

experience a loss of reputation. It's all part of the gamble.

John Cox Stevens, a wealthy American industrialist and founding member of the New York Yacht Club in the 1800s, was something of a gambler himself. A keen yachtsman who delighted in wagering large sums of money on the swiftness of his sailboats, he was also an ardent nationalist who demonstrably supported his country at every opportunity. When the British announced they would hold an international exposition in 1851 to celebrate worldwide progress in science, industry, and art, Stevens recognized an opportunity to show the world some of the significant advancements that his country's Industrial Revolution had yielded.

Stevens and five friends formed a syndicate that constructed, in the words of the builder, "a boat . . . faster than any vessel in the United States brought to compete with her." The name of the schooner, true to Stevens' nationalistic pride, was *America*.

Considerably different from British yachts, which were typically narrow and deep, *America* featured a sharp bow, wide beam, full stern, and low freeboard. Two steeply raked masts with no topsails and a single jib with no boom completed her look of an "out and outer," the term then

used to define true racing craft. When the 83-year-old Marquis of Anglesey closely inspected *America*, he uttered the now famous words, "If she is right, then all of us are wrong." That opinion, however, was not shared by English yachtsmen. When Stevens issued a challenge to any vessel of the Royal Yacht Squadron for a race in which he would wager the staggering amount of more than $50,000, there were no takers.

Instead, Stevens had to settle for a fleet race "open to yachts belonging to the clubs of all nations." The race offered a cash prize worth a little more than $500, accompanied by a rather ungainly silver trophy known as the Royal Yacht Squadron £100 Cup or the 100 Guineas Cup. Although called a cup, it was actually a bottomless ewer, or large water pitcher. The race drew seven schooners and eight cutters to the 53-mile course around the Isle of Wight on August 22, 1851. In front of thousands of spectators, *America* started last at 10:00 a.m. took the lead an hour and a half later; and by 5:50 p.m. she was 12 miles from the finish line and some seven and a half miles in front of *Aurora,* the second-place yacht. Almost three hours later, after the wind had died considerably, the race was over, and *America* took the honors, the cash, and the "cup."

The victory also prompted a near-legendary story.

Sir Thomas Lipton's Shamrock II crossed the finish line 2 seconds ahead of Columbia in the third race of the 1901 competition. Races at that time, however, were conducted under a handicap system and the defender was declared the winner on corrected time.

Although a number of historians dispute it ever happened, the story goes that Queen Victoria, aboard her royal yacht, asked who was winning the race. *"America,"* was the reply. When she asked who was next, the answer came back, "Your Majesty, there is no second." Myth or not, there are 29 skippers of America's Cup runners-up who would no doubt attest to the truth of the statement. Since then, the story of Queen Victoria's query about the status of the race has become synonymous with yacht racing in general, and to some extent with the fiercely competitive nature of yacht racers.

The cup *America* won was passed among the sailors for a while, but no one was quite sure what to do with it. Some suggested melting it down and making medallions out of the silver for distribution to the families of the men on board. Instead, the trophy was largely forgotten and stored away in an attic. In 1853 and 1857, Stevens, who held the position of Commodore at the New York Yacht Club, floated proposals for an international race, but nobody rose to the challenge. George Schuyler, a member of the original syndicate, recovered the cup from storage and presented it to the New York Yacht Club, calling it the "America's Cup." The trophy also came with what was called the Deed of Gift, a simple 239-word declaration of guidelines under which future races were to be run.

It wasn't until 1869 that the first challenge for the Cup was proposed. Englishman John Ashbury, challenging under the auspices of the Royal Thames Yacht Club, was combative, as so many challengers would prove to be. He took issue with the New Yorkers' choice of venue, their approval of the use of centerboard yachts, and their insistence that they had the right to field a fleet of yachts, rather than a single boat, to defend the trophy. Ashbury also claimed that the course in New York Harbor favored local knowledge, and he pushed for a race on more open water.

The New Yorkers rebutted each of Ashbury's arguments, and the debate raged until August 8, 1870, when 17 boats, including centerboarders, raced England's *Cambria* in New York Harbor. The English challenger finished a distant tenth, losing to the centerboarder *Magic.* Despite having had the right of way, *Cambria* had been forced to change course to avoid at least a half dozen of the club contenders. Ashbury refused to protest, however, even though his yacht had suffered damage during a collision. Most historians believe a protest would have been allowed and a rematch held.

Of note is the fact that the yacht *America* sailed in the race and reclaimed some of her now fading glory by finishing fourth. (It had been 19 years since her victory off the Isle of Wight.)

In 1871 James Ashbury was back knocking on the door of the New York Yacht Club, but this time he came prepared to meet the club on its own terms. Or at least he thought he came prepared. Following the disagreements over the previous year's racing conditions, the Englishman had consulted his lawyers, thus beginning a long tradition of legal involvement in a race that was supposed to be a friendly sporting endeavor.

As in the 1870 race, the issue of exactly what the word "match" meant was raised, a question that returned to haunt the event more than a century later. While in 1988 the question was actually sent to court for resolution, Ashbury and the New Yorkers avoided litigation. What they couldn't avoid, however, were bitter arguments and accusations of unsportsmanlike behavior by both sides.

Once the opposing parties finally got to sea, things didn't improve much. In fact, they got worse. In the second race, the race committee failed to inform the captain and crew aboard *Livonia,* Ashbury's challenger, that the course had been reduced by 10 miles. Nor did the officials issue instructions to the challenger on which side to round the marks, although this information was conveyed to the New York defenders. *Livonia* led at the first mark but lost the lead when she rounded the wrong way.

Ashbury protested and then refused to accept that the protest was disallowed. When *Livonia* won the third race fair and square, Ashbury announced he was now ahead 2–1, a claim also made by the defenders. When the latter won the next two races, the New Yorkers declared victory. Ashbury returned home empty-handed and accused the New York Yacht Club of being unfair and unsportsmanlike. In his later life, he emigrated to New Zealand and became a

Resolute, *seen here sailing along the waterfront in Bristol, Rhode Island, was the 1920 U.S. defender. Resolute's *victory against Lipton's* Shamrock IV *also marked the end of Herreshoff's extraordinary 27-year America's Cup career and the last time the Cup was raced in New York Harbor.*

Ranger (left, ripping through the water with Harold Vanderbilt at the wheel) was the last of the J-boats to defend the America's Cup and one of the most dominant racers of the 20th century, winning 32 of 34 races by an average of more than a mile per race. The yacht's design team included Rod and Olin Stephens as well as Drake Sparkman, principals in the design firm of Sparkman and Stephens, which created five successful 12-meter defenders.

sheep farmer and the first America's Cup skipper to live in that country.

In 1876 the Royal Canadian Yacht Club in Toronto forwarded a challenge to the New York Yacht Club. The defending club was overjoyed to accept, hoping for a new racing era in which it could display its understanding of fair play. Canada's 107-foot *Countess of Dufferin* was simply no match for *Madeleine*, the 106-foot speedster that won the two-out-of-three series by 11 and 27 minutes. Aside from the match proving America's superiority once again, the 1876 match was noteworthy for two other reasons: The boats did not start at anchor as in the previous two matches, and *Madeleine* was the only boat named for a woman to win and defend the trophy in the entire history of the America's Cup.

Canada challenged again in 1881, but the 70-foot *Atalanta* suffered the same fate as her predecessor. This time, the *American Mischief* won by 28 minutes and 39 minutes.

The result of the two lopsided victories was a revision of the Deed of Gift. Alexander Cuthbert, the owner and designer of *Countess of Dufferin* and *Atalanta*, announced he would once again challenge for the America's Cup in

1882. The New York Yacht Club, fearing the race's death by boredom, asked George Schuyler to revisit the original Deed and correct the problems that had arisen during the first four competitions. Schuyler added 263 words of more legalistic language to the Deed. Now the defender could enter only one boat, and the challenger who lost couldn't challenge again for two years. The new stipulations essentially put an end to Cuthbert's hopes of racing again in a year, and he went home. Meanwhile, the New York Yacht Club began searching for more prestigious challengers.

By 1885 Britain's Royal Yacht Squadron decided to win back the trophy it had lost to *America* in 1851. But to do so, it would have to beat the team headed by two Bostonians, owner Charles J. Paine and designer Edward Burgess. The races between the 94-foot *Puritan,* the first of three successful defenders designed by Burgess, and Britain's 96-foot *Genesta,* a classic narrow cutter design, went a long way toward repairing the faded profile of the event. The two boats were nearly equal in speed, although the final score was 2–0 in favor of the defender. In fact, in the final race, *Genesta* took the lead twice and actually led around the last mark before her opponent caught her in 30-knot winds on the final 15-mile beat to the finish. *Puritan* won by just 1 minute and 38 seconds.

Paine and Burgess worked their magic again in 1886 and 1887; this was the only period in Cup history that the event was run three years in a row. In 1886, *Mayflower* beat the Royal Yacht Squadron's *Galatea* by more than 12 and 29 minutes in two races, and the following year *Volunteer* took out Scotland's Royal Clyde Yacht Club's entry

Thistle by more than 19 and 11 minutes.

There had now been seven America's Cup matches, and seven times the defender had won easily. But the New York Yacht Club was still uncomfortable with the rules of the game, and they again revised the Deed of Gift. Perhaps the biggest change made was that the document now called for races to be held on the ocean—the venue of New York Harbor had raised the hackles of more than one challenger—over alternating triangle and windward-leeward 30-mile courses.

From 1893 to 1930, two men took center stage in the America's Cup matches and brought with them a brilliance and dignity perhaps unique in the Cup's history. Nathanael Herreshoff's dominating reign of excellence began with the design of V*igilant,* a 124-foot monster sloop that required 70 crewmen to handle her. The designer himself proved the only capable helmsman of this unique vessel, and he steered her to three straight victories over the Earl of Dunraven's *Valkyrie II.* Dunraven, representing the Royal Yacht Squadron, was as argumentative a challenger as any of his predecessors. In 1895, when his *Valkyrie III* lost to Herreshoff's *Defender,* Dunraven accused the New York Yacht Club of fraud after a race in which he finished first was disqualified due to a foul at the start.

What came to be known as the Dunraven Affair ended ingloriously in 1896 when the Earl was expelled from his honorary membership in the New York Yacht Club. With this dismissal came the end of any hopes of another English challenge in the near future, and club members began to wonder if the event was worth the rancor and disputes it

seemed to engender.

Three years later, however, a Scotsman by way of America and Ireland brought light to the darkest days of the America's Cup. Thomas Lipton was born in 1850 to impoverished Irish parents living in Glasgow, Scotland. As a boy he emigrated to the United States and eventually worked in a New York grocery store. At 19 he returned to Scotland and opened his own grocery store, which soon became a chain of stores and later an international success.

In 1899, as Sir Thomas Lipton, he made the first of his five legendary challenges for the Cup on behalf of Ireland's Royal Ulster Yacht Club. Although he lost all of them, four times to Herreshoff-designed vessels, Lipton brought an unwavering sense of sportsmanship that was previously unknown in America's Cup competition. Naming each of his boats *Shamrock* (*I* through V), Lipton was an innovator who was the first to tank-test a scale model, in 1901, before building a racing yacht. Yet his inventiveness was matched by Herreshoff's brilliance, and Lipton's money was overmatched by syndicates that included J. Pierpont Morgan, William Rockefeller, and Cornelius Vanderbilt.

It wasn't until 1920, in his fourth challenge with his fourth *Shamrock,* that Sir Thomas managed to win his first race. In fact, he won the first two against Herreshoff's sixth

After a 19-year hiatus in Cup competition, the match in 1958 heralded the advent of the smaller, more affordable 12-meter boats. In the first color photograph of Cup action, Columbia is pictured at left, having just beaten the Royal Yacht Squadron's Sceptre. Columbia's designer, naval architect Olin Stephens, syndicate manager Henry Sears, and skipper Briggs Cunningham (right, left to right respectively) admire their handiwork.

and final America's Cup boat, *Resolute.* Needing only one more win to capture the Cup, *Shamrock IV* actually crossed the finish line ahead of her opponent in the third race, but these races were conducted under a handicap system: Smaller boats with less sail area were allowed additional time. In the third race, Lipton's yacht owed *Resolute* 7 minutes and 1 second, and the defender was therefore awarded the race. Lipton's heart must have broken as the Americans won the final two races easily. He may have been somewhat consoled, however, by the knowledge that in the thirteen America's Cup matches to date, his challenge had come closest to taking the trophy home.

Resolute's victory marked the end of Nathanael Herreshoff's extraordinary 27-year America's Cup career. His contributions to the event and to the world of yacht design were vast. His *Reliance*, at 144 feet with 16,000 square feet of sail, was the largest boat ever to sail in the America's Cup—and some say the ugliest. His *Columbia* was the first of only three boats (*Intrepid* and *Courageous* were the other two) to successfully defend twice in a row, and some say she was the most beautiful of all Cup boats. His "Universal Rule," a rating system for boats, revolutionized not only America's Cup racing but to some extent yacht racing

throughout the world. His legacy is not only one of brilliance but one of preserving and representing what the original members of the America syndicate had in mind when they created the competition: the pursuit of technical excellence.

Sir Thomas Lipton's fifth and final challenge came in 1930, 31 years after his first *Shamrock* joined the battle. Throughout those years Lipton had displayed an uncommon grace and elegance in losing yacht races, but he had won the hearts of an international audience, and at age 80 he was still game. His fifth *Shamrock* was well designed and sailed fast, but the defender's *Enterprise* was technologically superior. William Starling Burgess, Edward's son, designed the U.S. boat. Harold Vanderbilt was the skipper of *Enterprise,* which won 4–0. But because he defeated the man who many credit with saving the America's Cup, Vanderbilt found no joy in victory. "Our hour of triumph, our hour of victory is all but at hand," he wrote. "But it is so tempered with sadness that it is almost hollow . . . ." His

The 1962 Cup elicited the first Australian challenger in Gretel, which was just barely defeated by Constellation (opposite, right and left respectively). The '64 match proved more decisive as the British challenger Sovereign (above) lost soundly to Constellation by an average of 12 minutes.

sentiments were shared by millions around the globe.

The 1930 match saw the debut of the J-class sloops, the graceful beauties that preceded the "modern era" of America's Cup yachts and are today a symbol of the big, powerful vessels owned by the wealthy and raced for the thrill of it. The *Enterprise/Shamrock V* match was also the first to be conducted in the waters off Newport, Rhode

The Australians returned in 1967 to challenge **Intrepid.** *To their chagrin,* **Dame Pattie** *was routed 4–0.* **Intrepid** *(featured at right with its 1970 Cup-winning team) was one of Stephens' most radical designs, introducing an extremely small keel, among other innovations.*

Island, where the New York Yacht Club would defend the Cup for the next 53 years.

The J-boat era was shortlived, with only the 1934 and 1937 matches raced in that class. After the death of Lipton, British aviation magnate T. O. M. Sopwith rose to the challenge, and his *Endeavour* came as close to winning the Cup in 1934 as any boat since *Shamrock IV* and closer than any challenger to follow until *Australia II* accomplished the task in 1983. The 1934 America's Cup race was the first to no longer use time allowances. Matched against *Rainbow,* designed by W. S. Burgess, *Endeavour* won the first match by 2 minutes and 9 seconds. *Endeavour* came back with a 51-second victory in race two. Race three was the turning point of the match. Sopwith had a six-minute lead at the final mark and needed only to steer a straight course to the finish line on a 15-mile reach. But he panicked, tacked to cover his opponent, and *Rainbow* blew by. After that the defender won the next three races to keep the Cup.

Sopwith was back in 1937 with *Endeavour II,* but Burgess was also back, leading a team of designers who included Olin and Rod Stephens and Drake Sparkman. The result of their collaboration was *Ranger,* the last of the J-boats to defend the America's Cup and one of the most dominant racers of the 20th century. In the summer of

1937, the great yacht won 32 of 34 races by an average of more than a mile per race. Sopwith was sent home without a victory in four attempts, leading skipper Vanderbilt to declare that the yacht was so powerful that no further competition would be found and the J-class era would end. The prediction was correct: The coming of World War II, and with it a decline in interest in America's Cup competition, temporarily diminished the now 86-year-old event's popularity.

Once world peace was restored, however, and prosperity became the goal of the 1950s, at least in America, the New York Yacht Club began to search out interest in renewing the "Holy Grail of yacht racing." The search was also on for another type of boat. Even the most die-hard traditionalists realized that the days of the 100-footers were over, and they settled on the 12-meter. A popular boat first built in 1906, the narrow-beamed craft with a more definitive V-shaped hull was adopted by the New York Yacht Club as the new America's Cup racer, and the club once more revised the Deed of Gift. This fourth document, validated by the Supreme Court of New York in 1956, contained two new provisions. One of them read, "The competing yachts or vessels, if one mast, shall not be less than forty-four feet nor more than ninety feet on the load waterline." The other provision dropped the requirement that boats had to sail to the venue on their own bottoms.

If the new yacht and new rules gave potential challengers any impression that the defender might now be more vulnerable to defeat, that notion was quickly dispelled during the 1958 match between the New York Yacht Club's *Columbia* and the Royal Yacht Squadron's *Sceptre*. Designed by Olin Stephens, *Columbia* won every start but one. Of more importance, she left *Sceptre* to her stern at the finish line by an average of eight minutes in the four official races. (Race two was thrown out when the time limit expired.)

Four years later, the 1962 match brought new blood to the America's Cup when the Royal Sydney Yacht Squadron challenged. The first Down Under effort was a strong one. *Gretel*, designed by Alan Payne with the aid of American testing tanks and outfitted with U.S. sail material and winches, won the second race and lost the fourth by just 26 seconds. Credit is given to defending helmsman Bus Mosbacher aboard *Weatherly* for employing tactics that kept the Cup bolted in the New York clubhouse, even though the Australian boat was widely believed to be faster.

The fact that this was the first time since the 1934 match that a challenger had won a race made an impression on the New Yorkers. They quickly revisited the rules and issued a "country-of-origin" interpretation. Simply stated, this declaration demanded that challengers use facilities, products, and personnel that were native to their country.

By 1970, after defender *Constellation* easily beat the

In 1977, Courageous (leading Australia at left)
beat Australia's fifth America's Cup challenge 4–0.
Dressed in yachting white, Baron Bich (right)
brought a Gallic sense of style to the America's
Cup as the backer of the French challenges
between 1970 and 1983.

British Sovereign in 1964 by an average winning margin of 12-plus minutes, and *Intrepid* subsequently went undefeated against Australia's *Dame Pattie* in 1967, the New York Yacht Club had successfully defended the America's Cup in 20 matches over 97 years.

A century after the first America's Cup, the first multinational challenge occurred in 1970 when clubs from Greece, Britain, France, and Australia entered the competition. Greece and Britain dropped out before the challenger trials, leaving Australia's *Gretel II*, owned by Sir Frank Packard, to fight it out with *France*, owned by Baron Marcel Bich. The Australians prevailed and were able to win one race in the Cup match against a modified *Intrepid*. The 4–1 score belies the closeness of the match. Many believed that closeness was a result of the challenger trials, which provided an opportunity for skippers to tune their boats and battle-test their sailors.

In 1974, the New Yorkers received seven challenges, but only France and Australia built boats. Australia again beat France for the right to race the defender. The 4–0 score in favor of *Courageous* over Australia's *Southern Cross* continued the American winning streak. The event was also noteworthy as the debut of the four most often discussed America's Cup participants: Australia's Alan Bond and Bob Miller (who later changed his name to Ben

Lexcen) and America's Ted Turner and Dennis Conner.

In 1977, the defender trials featured the sport's two most accomplished and famous sailmakers, Ted Hood and Lowell North. Hood designed and skippered *Independence;* North's boat was *Enterprise.* But *Courageous* got the nod from the yacht club's selection committee, and at her helm this time was Ted Turner, the ascendant media mogul who later married Academy Award-winning actress Jane Fonda. Turner's tactician was Gary Jobson, who built his own career in television as ESPN's sailing commentator. Bond was back as the challenger, and although his *Australia* lost to *Courageous* 4–0, the margin of victory in each race was less than three minutes.

By 1980, 37-year-old Dennis Conner had compiled one of the most impressive yacht racing records in the world. Two-time world champion in the competitive Star class and winner of the Olympic bronze medal in the Tempest class, the San Diego, California, native proved his match racing abilities as champion of the Congressional Cup regatta and as the starting helmsman and tactician aboard *Courageous* in 1974. Conner marshaled all his talents and his considerable organizational skills in his *Freedom* campaign. In the defense trials he won 36 of 40 races against Turner, who returned with *Courageous,* and against Russell Long, who entered *Clipper.*

The challenger trials featured boats from Sweden, Britain, France, and Australia. Once again, the finals came down to a battle between the teams led by Baron Bich and Alan Bond. The victorious Australian team advanced to the America's Cup match, but they won only one race against Conner and his crew.

Freedom was the last America's Cup defender designed by Olin Stephens. Even in this day and age of computer-assisted boat designs, design teams numbering more than a dozen people, and in some cases unlimited budgets, Stephens' record of producing fast boats remains unequaled. Beginning with his work on *Ranger* in 1937 and continuing through the 12-meter era with *Columbia* (1958), *Constellation* (1964), *Intrepid* (1967), *Courageous* (1974 and 1977), and, finally, *Freedom* (1980), Stephens influenced not only America's Cup boat design but boat design in general. No other person before or since, with the possible exception of Nathanael Herreshoff, was comparable to Stephens. He was a giant in the field and will remain a legend in America's Cup circles for as long as the regatta is run.

The 1983 match between Conner's *Liberty* and *Australia II,* designed by Ben Lexcen, bankrolled by Alan Bond, and skippered by John Bertrand, was the watershed event in the then 132-year history of the America's Cup. It brought more attention to the competition than ever before and introduced the now famous "wing keel" as a design concept that some consider the single most innovative advancement in modern Cup history.

The Australians had to battle the British, Canadians, French, and Italians (new to the event) to win the chal-

1977's Courageous was skippered by the future media tycoon, Ted Turner. Standing at the helm (right), the flamboyant Turner is credited with attracting public attention to the America's Cup with his colorful—some said outrageous—style.

Freedom (in rough seas at left in 1980) was the last boat designed by the venerable Olin Stephens. It was also skippered by Conner, who possessed one of the most impressive yacht racing records in the world. Conner won 36 of 40 races against Ted Turner, securing the right to defend the Cup against the persistent Australians.

lenger's berth. Conner's archrival, Tom Blackaller, teamed with Gary Jobson in the *Defender* campaign, which joined forces with a newly formed Courageous syndicate in an effort to depose the San Diego skipper.

By now, costs to campaign an America's Cup 12-meter had escalated astronomically. Conner had pushed the on-the-water testing and crew training envelope to include a two-year program. Monthly costs for food, housing, salaries, and sail and hull development, among many other items, were estimated at $200,000 per month. Masts cost between $50,000 and $70,000. Exotic materials like Kevlar and Mylar had made their way into sailcloth and increased costs considerably. But even so, 1983 costs were minor when compared to the checks being written for the 1999/2000 campaigns.

On the challenger side, *Australia II* proved to be the superboat that the New York Yacht Club had long feared. Before meeting Britain's *Victory* in the challenger finals, the Australian boat had amassed a 44–5 record and then advanced to the America's Cup match with a 4–1 defeat of the Brits.

Conner's road to the Cup was not as clear-cut as the Australians. He had commissioned two new boats to be built and had chosen the red-hulled *Liberty*, designed by Johan Valentijn, to go to war. *Courageous*, now skippered by Cup newcomer John Kolius, was 10 years old, but her 6–5 performance in the preliminary defender round proved just how great a boat she was. *Defender* ended that round at 5–6, and *Liberty* was 5–5.

Between rounds all three boats returned to the shed for substantial modifications, and *Liberty* began to emerge as the favorite. In the defender finals, *Defender* could do no better than a 1–9 record and was eliminated. *Liberty* then disposed of *Courageous*, and the most famous match in all of America's Cup history was set: Dennis Conner at the helm of *Liberty* versus John Bertrand steering *Australia II*.

When *Liberty* won the first two races, the fears of the yacht club were somewhat abated. But gear breakage on *Australia II* had as much to do with her defeat as Conner's skills or *Liberty's* speed. In race three, the Australian superboat gave an indication of just how super she was. Her margin of victory was 3 minutes and 14 seconds, the largest margin ever posted by a challenger. Conner and crew sailed flawlessly in race four to win by just 43 seconds. Now on the verge of victory, the red boat needed just one more win.

Bertrand was over early at the start in race five. But gear failure on *Liberty* and the sheer speed of *Australia II* gave him the lead on the first leg, a lead he never lost. Race six became a matter of Bertrand finding wind when Conner couldn't, and again the Australians turned a deficit into a lead and went on to win by 3 minutes and 25 seconds.

With the score now tied, the two boats met for the

deciding race on September 26. Conner opted for a timed start rather than mixing it up with his more maneuverable opponent. The strategy paid off with an 8-second lead across the starting line. Both boats then went in search of wind shifts. *Australia II* caught the first and surged to the lead, only to watch *Liberty* regain it when the shift favored the defender.

Conner maintained the lead and rounded the windward mark 29 seconds ahead. Bertrand's crew changed to a lighter spinnaker on the first downwind run and

*The Australians arrived at Newport for their fifth America's Cup match determined to take the Cup home. Upon arrival, **Australia II** wore a "modesty skirt" to cover her top-secret and controversial "wing keel." Above, designer Ben Lexcen gleefully balanced himself against the technical breakthrough that may have been the difference in the Aussie triumph. Conner's **Liberty** (opposite, left) maneuvered against John Bertrand's **Australia II** (right) in the bright Rhode Island sun.*

After a neck-and-neck race, Australia II *sailed across the finish line 41 seconds ahead of Conner's red-hulled* Liberty. *The longest winning streak in the history of world sport was over. It had taken seven attempts and 21 years, but the Cup finally belonged to Australia. The smiling faces of skipper John Bertrand and syndicate owner Alan Bond (opposite, left and right respectively) attested to the joy of victory.*

made up 22 seconds. Now with just seven seconds between the two, it was back to searching for shifts. Conner placed his boat in the right place at the right time and opened up a 57-second advantage around the third mark.

It now appeared that the defender had a substantial enough lead to carry him through the next three legs. But as the first run had shown, *Australia II* was a speedboat downwind. She began to recover some distance on the second run, forcing Conner to decide either to cover his opponent and ultimately wage a jibing duel, or to jibe off to the left-hand side of the course to find the wind that had earlier served him so well.

His decision to jibe will be debated around yacht club bars for eternity, and no doubt it has caused Conner more than one sleepless night. As Bertrand went to starboard, the wind went with him and pushed him into a 21-second lead at the leeward mark. Despite Conner's desperate 47-tack final beat, *Australia II* stretched her lead and sailed across the finish line 41 seconds ahead of the red boat. History was made. The longest winning streak in the history of world sport was over.

From Plastic to Silver

CHAPTER TWO

FROM PLASTIC TO SILVER

Before the great Australian upset of 1983, few New Zealanders paid the America's Cup much attention; for them, the Olympic Games were considered the ultimate challenge. The fact that Australia's win electrified the victor's nation and brought both pride and dollars flowing Down Under did not go unnoticed across the Tasman Sea. All of a sudden there was an "If they can do it, why can't we" attitude among Kiwis that was whispered about in yacht clubs and corporate boardrooms. And the more the question was asked, the more the answer "We can" took on full voice.

Smashing through a wave, Dennis Conner's Stars & Stripes successfully challenged the Australians for the Cup in 1987. Buoyed by the race "Down Under," New Zealand also joined the competition for the first time. Their fiberglass upstart, Kiwi Magic, made it to the final challenger trials, losing 4–1 to Stars & Stripes.

In many yachting circles throughout the world it is commonly believed that Sir Michael Fay initiated the original challenge idea and championed it until it became a reality. Yet, according to Fay, the man who actually launched New Zealand into America's Cup orbit was a Belgian futures and commodities trader named Marcel Fachler. Based in Sydney, Fachler was an eyewitness to Australia's extravagant reaction to winning the Cup. And apparently he believed his own business interests would be well served if he entered a challenge through the Royal New Zealand Yacht Squadron for the 1986-87 America's Cup.

Fachler's challenge took the yachting world by surprise, particularly the Royal New Zealand Yacht Squadron. It seems the Belgian neglected to officially advise the Squadron of his plans, and the Kiwi yachtsmen discovered their involvement only by reading the morning newspa-

per. Fachler soon suffered business reversals and effectively disappeared. Michael Fay, then a 37-year-old merchant banker, stepped into the breach.

Fay put together a plan that included two critical decisions, both of which had a significant impact on the entire campaign: to build identical boats out of fiberglass and to enter the 12-meter World Championships in Fremantle, Australia, in February 1986.

Since 1958, when 12-meter yachts were first used in the America's Cup, every defender and challenger had built their racers out of wood or aluminum. Other designers had considered fiberglass but rejected it because it was costly and could not be reshaped, cut, or welded like aluminum. But fiberglass has several advantages over aluminum. It won't bend and buckle in heavy seas under the huge loads large yachts generate, which can cause a loss of boat speed. Also, a fiberglass boat is lighter than a boat of the same size made of aluminum. But the real genius of the idea for the Kiwis was that two boats made from the same fiberglass mold at the same time would be identical and would also be less expensive to produce than two aluminum boats built at different times.

By using two identical boats to test sails, keels, rudders, and even entire teams, the New Zealanders knew immediately what worked and what didn't. Two-boat programs had been used in the past, but because the boats were

When New Zealand attempted to bring back the golden age of yachting with its 1988 "Big Boat" challenge to the San Diego Yacht Club, Dennis Conner responded with a 60-foot catamaran (left), resulting in an absurd mismatch (right) and a bitter legal battle.

never identical, there was no true way of knowing whether what was being tested made the difference or whether the difference was inherent in the designs of the two boats. Producing identical boats was one of the most significant design advancements in modern America's Cup history and one that would pay enormous returns for New Zealand just nine years later.

By the time the 1986 12-meter World Championship was held, the first two of three fiberglass boats were built. When the final scores were posted and Chris Dickson aboard *KZ-5* was listed in second place behind *Australia III*, eyebrows met hairlines throughout the world of sail-

boat racing. Who was this kid? What was this boat? Where the hell was New Zealand?

The 26th edition of the America's Cup regatta began with the challenger trials on October 5, 1986. The event was especially notable for the many firsts it recorded: first time the United States was not the defender; first time as many as 13 teams, representing six nations, were entered; first time New Zealand had made a challenge; first time television cameras were allowed on board the racing vessels; first time a fiberglass boat was racing.

The America's Cup debut of the fiberglass yacht was auspicious, to say the least. In the first round-robin of the challenger trials, New Zealand's record was 11–1; the only loss was to Dennis Conner's *Stars & Stripes*. Conner had lost in 1983 to *Australia II* with her famous, some say infamous, wing keel, and his actions in 1986 proved he had arrived in Fremantle determined to dispute any and all design elements he considered outside the rules. Throughout the trials Conner focused especially on the fiberglass issue. Asked at a press conference what he thought about the plastic boat, Conner blurted out, "The last 78 12-meters built around the world have been built in aluminum, so why would you build one in fiberglass unless you wanted to cheat?" This opinion was immediately met with a firestorm of criticism from New Zealanders aimed at Conner.

"Glassgate," as the media loved to call the affair, may have generated a good deal of sound and fury on land, but it was of no consequence on the water. Going into the finals, *Kiwi Magic* had beaten *Stars & Stripes* two of the three times they raced and had now compiled a record of 37-1. *Stars & Stripes* stood at 31-7. On paper, and indeed on the water, the New Zealanders looked invincible, but Conner proved he was still the master of the game by sending the Kiwis home, 4-1. On the defender side, Alan Bond's campaign to defend the trophy his team had won in Newport three years earlier had come unglued. *Australia IV* lost to *Kookaburra III*, campaigned by the syndicate headed by Bond's archrival Kevin Parry and steered by Iain Murray. It was a bitter contest on and off the water.

In the Cup match *Stars & Stripes* enjoyed a decisive

After 1988, the IACC set down regulations for the new generation of yachts seen here. These sleek speed machines—stretching some 75 feet, with 70 percent more sail area and weighing 30 percent less—changed the face of Cup racing. Bow to bow with **Team New Zealand** *(left), the Italian* **Il Moro di Venezia** *triumphed at the Louis Vuitton trials.*

4–0 victory over *Kookaburra III*, winning by an average margin of 1 minute and 39 seconds. The trophy that had spent so many years in the United States was headed north, to San Diego, California.

While the yacht racing world waited for details of the 27th America's Cup, Michael Fay delivered a formal "Big Boat" challenge to the commodore of the San Diego Yacht Club, based on his interpretation of the Deed of Gift. Fay noted that the Deed of Gift encourages challengers to initiate a competition as long as they meet certain criteria, one of them being that the waterline length of the boat in which they are challenging be no less than 44 feet or no more than 90 feet. Fay envisioned a glorious battle of behemoths. Monohulls more than 130 feet in length overall would recall the golden age of yachting but would be built with the advanced technologies and materials of the modern day. Fay's vision wasn't shared by the San Diego Yacht Club, and his challenge initiated the most bitter, controversial, and litigious episode in America's Cup history.

The argument eventually went to the Supreme Court of New York, the legal custodian of the Deed of Gift. On November 25, 1987, Judge Carmen Beauchamp Ciparick ruled that the challenge was legal, and she disallowed the San Diego Yacht Club's request to make 12-meter yachts

standard. The shocker came when Dennis Conner announced he would meet the New Zealand "Big Boat" challenge in a 60-foot catamaran. Back to court went New Zealand requesting that San Diego be ordered to defend the Cup in a 90-foot waterline boat. This time Judge Ciparick ruled that New Zealand's suit was premature. In essence she said go race, and if you have protests, come back and see me.

So they raced in 1988—a giant monohull, dragging tons of keel through the ocean, against a multihull craft that skimmed over the water's surface. It was a mismatch played out to a foregone conclusion. The catamaran won by more than 18 and 20 minutes in the two races. When the races ended, it was back to court to see the judge. The yachting world in general agreed with the opinions of the Royal Perth Yacht Club and the New York Yacht Club, the two previous trustees of the America's Cup. In separate opinions submitted to the court, both clubs wrote that they believed the current races did not constitute a match as the term was used in the Deed of Gift.

Judge Ciparick ruled in favor of New Zealand, but that ruling was soon overturned by the New York Court of Appeals. The Kiwis were forced to return once again to San Diego in 1992 if they wanted to try to win the Cup on the water.

In the space of a little more than one year, the America's Cup had gone from the zenith it achieved in Fremantle to the nadir it reached in San Diego. While all the squabbling and litigation was going on, America's Cup officials took steps to prevent future mismatches. The

International America's Cup Class (IACC) was established, together with design parameters for the new boat to be used in the races. Although 12-meter yachts had been the America's Cup standard for almost 30 years, by 1988 they were perceived as too heavy and short on sail area. The IACC boats—at 75 feet, with 70 percent more sail area and 30 percent less weight—were promoted as speed machines. They made their racing debut at the 1991 World Championships in San Diego, the warmup for the America's Cup scheduled for the following year.

A newcomer to the competition in 1992 was American multimillionaire Bill Koch, whose America[3] syndicate was out to dethrone Dennis Conner as the Cup defender. Italian industrialist Raul Gardini headed up his country's challenging syndicate, with American Paul Cayard as skipper and helmsman. Japan's Nippon Challenge was a first-time challenger, as was the team from Spain. Back in the fray were teams from France, Sweden, and Australia, with two syndicates.

By now it seemed that an America's Cup couldn't be run without a design controversy. The wing keel, the fiberglass issue, and the Big Boat all caused consternation from a rules perspective. In 1992 it was the great bowsprit debate over the legality of the New Zealand boat's foremost appendage, designed to make trimming and jibing the giant asymmetrical spinnaker easier. The Italians led the attack throughout the challenger round robins. The debate grew hotter still when the warring principals, Italy and New Zealand, advanced to the Louis Vuitton Cup finals.

With American Rod Davis at the helm, the Kiwis jumped out to a 4–1 lead and needed only one more victory to advance to the America's Cup match. But not so fast! During the fifth race, as Cayard trailed by more than two minutes and saw the desperate situation his Italian team was in, he chose to raise the protest flag and with it, the bowsprit issue yet again.

The Louis Vuitton jury ruled in favor of the Italian protest and chose to "annul" the Kiwis' fourth victory. Suddenly the New Zealand lead was cut from 4–1 to 3–1. The victory in the protest room fired up the Italians and unsettled the Kiwis. For some 35 races the New Zealanders had used the bowsprit and now, suddenly, they had to use whole new techniques to carry out the same sail-handling functions. The Kiwi camp was in disarray, and their offensive collapsed. The Italians swept the next four races for a 5–3 victory. Three times the Kiwis had entered the America's Cup, and three times they had been involved in bitter, controversial defeats.

In the defender competition, Bill Koch's America[3] team defeated reigning champion Dennis Conner. Koch reportedly spent $64 million of his own money in an effort that at its core was based on science and technology. Whether he owed his victory to money, superior technology, organization, preparation, or just plain old sailing skills is a subject for yacht club bar discussions. But there

is little doubt that the two teams who vied for the Cup in 1992 were the biggest spenders. Estimates of the Italians' war chest topped $100 million.

America[3] won the match against *Il Moro di Venezia* 4–1 with superior boat speed, both successfully defending the America's Cup and dictating that the next event would be in San Diego.

The 1995 event was unlike any of the America's Cup regattas that had preceded it. Exciting the most interest was the all-women's team that Bill Koch and his *America*[3] syndicate had selected to defend the trophy. Only three women had raced in earlier America's Cup matches, and all three had served as timekeepers. The last Cup match in which a woman participated was in 1937. Since then three other women had sailed in trial matches, but not in the America's Cup proper.

The all-women's team attracted a boatload of press clippings from around the world, but so too did the possible rematch of John Bertrand and Dennis Conner. Bertrand had come back from yacht-racing retirement after his '83 defeat by the U.S. skipper to head the oneAustralia syndicate. Japan, France, and Spain were competing again, and, with two challenges from Australia and two from New Zealand, the challenger armada numbered seven. On the defense, a group from Maine called PACT '95 was, along with Conner, attempting to unseat *America*[3], the defending champion.

Team New Zealand, with Russell Coutts at the helm of the yacht that was never officially named but became known as *Black Magic,* began to demonstrate the most

dominating performance in America's Cup history in the early rounds of the challenger trials.

Yet despite Team New Zealand's history-making achievement, the day of March 5, 1995—which may live forever as the Day of Infamy in America's Cup history— overshadowed the challenger races. Team New Zealand was racing *oneAustralia* that day. On the second beat to windward tragedy struck, and in the immortal words of John Bertrand responding to a press conference question, "The boat broke in half and sank. That's what happened."

Worldwide, front page headlines told the story of how *oneAustralia* had just come off a series of waves when the sailors on board heard a crack. The boat appeared to break transversely behind the main primary winches. It was the worst disaster in the regatta's history, but all the sailors were rescued. To this day a number of theories abound as to exactly why the sinking occurred. All that is really known is that the boat, representing some 20,000 hours of labor, energy, and heart, still lies at the bottom of the Pacific Ocean. The team continued to compete by racing its second boat.

On the defender's course, PACT '95's yacht *Young America* finished the four round-robins with 14 wins. Dennis Conner's *Stars & Stripes* posted 11 victories, while the all-women team (now with a man on board) had

Bill Koch, multimillionaire and owner of the America[3] syndicate, is held aloft by his 1995 all-women's team. An historic first for the traditionally male bastion of the America's Cup, the women's team made it to the defender's semifinals. Team New Zealand (right) lost to Italy in a challenger finals marred by controversy.

recorded 5 wins. Then in the semifinals, *Young America* continued her winning ways with 9 wins in 10 races, while the women's team finished the series with 4 victories, one more than *Stars & Stripes.*

It appeared that the finals in the defense trials would be raced between *America[3]* and *Young America,* but in one of the most bizarre surprises in yachting history, a deal was struck between the three defense teams to race all three boats in what had always been a two-boat final.

Escaping elimination after coming in third in the semifinals was an extraordinary, if peculiar, break for Conner. But it was the outcome of his final race in the defender trials against the women's team that could turn even the most ardent skeptic of destiny into a true believer. When the women rounded the final mark and headed for the finish line some 44 lengths ahead of Conner, it seemed

New Zealand's Russell Coutts (right) skippered Black Magic to its overwhelming 1995 victory over Conner's Stars & Stripes. Team New Zealand's involvement in the Cup competition had begun a scant 12 years earlier. Having won the right to host Cup 2000 in Auckland, the Kiwis have invited the challengers to practice there against their 1992 boats (left).

certain they would advance to the Cup match. But it's not for nothing that Dennis Conner is called "Mr. America's Cup," and as the women sailed into a hole *Stars & Stripes* caught a freshening breeze and overtook her stalled opponent. Dennis had done it again. For the third time in the past four America's Cups, he would be racing New Zealand, which had completed the Louis Vuitton Cup with a remarkable 37–1 record.

But Conner's magic ended there; he couldn't contend with *Black Magic*. The Kiwis' 5–0 sweep was the greatest margin of victory in the 144-year history of the Cup. *Black Magic* led at all 30 marks in the five races, gaining time on 25 of the legs and winning by an average of 2 minutes and 52 seconds in each race. The 42–1 overall record was the best ever posted by any America's Cup team. The Kiwis gained time over the opposition in 77 percent of the 260 legs they raced, and they were in the lead on 93 percent of those legs.

The victory brought the America's Cup to Auckland, where Team New Zealand will defend it beginning in February 2000. The team that races the Kiwis will come from a field of 13 challengers that begin competing for the Louis Vuitton Cup in October 1999.

A Perfect Venue

CHAPTER THREE

A PERFECT VENUE

Auckland, New Zealand, will be only the fifth venue in America's Cup history to host the regatta. During the 132 years that the United States successfully defended the Cup, all of the matches since 1930 took place in Newport, Rhode Island. America's Cup sailing and Newport became so well connected that they were considered a permanent institution by many boating enthusiasts, and indeed many of the competitors.

Whenever the event was staged people would travel to Newport not only to watch or compete in the action on the

Picturesque Auckland will become the fifth venue to host the America's Cup. It is hard to imagine a more appropriate site—through its success on the water as well as its boat-building, spar and sail-making industries, New Zealand has developed a worldwide reputation and is recognized as one of the best places in the world to build and race a high-performance yacht.

water, but also to enjoy some of the fabled parties that have become synonymous with the America's Cup social whirl. Hosting and attending lavish affairs celebrating the yachting lifestyle and promoting the uniqueness of international sport's oldest trophy became de rigueur among both residents and competitors. Certain invitations on land became as prized as victories at sea. After all, Newport had long established itself as the summer playground of the very rich and famous. Here was home to the mansions of the Astors and the Vanderbilts. Jack Kennedy squired Jackie Bouvier about town and married her on the grounds of an estate overlooking America's Cup waters.

The town is proud of its link to the event. The main street is named America's Cup Avenue. Photographs and memorabilia of past contests are still found in many of the bars and restaurants. The house where successful Australian skipper John Bertrand was said to have resided dur-

Once a small run-down fishing port, Fremantle became the colorful Australian host to the 1987 America's Cup. Enthusiastic crowds gathered to welcome the challenger, Dennis Conner's Stars & Stripes (opposite). Though the trophy room in the New York Yacht Club on 44th Street in Manhattan (left) has seemed bare since the Australians first made off with the spoils, the club has remained a bustling hub for the U.S. campaign to wrest the Cup back from the New Zealanders in 2000.

ing 1983 has a simple plaque on the front door reading "John Bertrand's House." When it was Cup time, Newport was transformed. A good part of its economy revolved around the America's Cup.

But since Bertrand and Bond and their band of Aussies left town with the Cup, the small New England town has not been quite the same. While still a seafaring town in many respects and still host to many prestigious regattas, Newport without the Cup is like London without its bridge. The New York Yacht Club, which for more than a century conducted its business within the concrete confines of Manhattan, purchased a mansion on Newport Harbor and now has a clubhouse and dock to which members can actually bring their boats. The New York City building is still active, although the trophy room where the America's Cup was encased for so many years now seems bare without it.

When the event moved to Fremantle, Australia, it took on another flavor. The Australians built a special America's Cup yacht harbor to house all of the challenging and defending teams. Fremantle, previously a small run-down fishing port, was transformed overnight into a colorful, vibrant village spilling over with activity. The town developed an America's Cup village atmosphere where competitors, supporters, spectators, and media could all share stories and mix with each other. If Newport had about it the feel of the aristocracy, Fremantle opened its doors to the common man. All were welcome, and all welcomed the atmosphere.

Just eight miles from the lively city of Perth in Western Australia, Fremantle sits hard by the Indian Ocean. As a venue for the America's Cup, it benefited from prevailing strong winds, dubbed the Fremantle Doctor, which seemed to appear every day about noon, as the boats made their way to the race course. The conditions at sea consistently challenged the teams like never before and provided perhaps the best television footage in sailing history. The racing was spectacular, and the event grew in popularity.

The Fremantle era was shortlived as Dennis Conner and his team aboard *Stars & Stripes* put on a masterful display of boat preparation and racing skills to win back the Cup for the United States in 1987. Conner took the trophy and the regatta to San Diego, his hometown.

Unlike Newport or Fremantle, small towns that offered more intimate settings, the city of San Diego did not develop a central base for the syndicates, which were spread over a 10-mile radius. The membership of the San Diego Yacht Club did their best to progress the event, but with no central location, they were unable to create the same village atmosphere. And no doctor made afternoon house calls as the light Southern California winds meant that the racing and the television footage was dull in comparison to

New Zealand's original Maori inhabitants viewed the island as a Garden of Eden because of its abundant wildlife, joined today by a thriving population of sheep (left). Mount Cook of Southern Island (right) further testifies to the country's spectacular natural beauty.

Fremantle. And after the debacle of the big boat versus catamaran episode that dragged the Cup through the courts, the 1992 and 1995 regattas in San Diego had lost some of their luster. Many who started out with high hopes for the event in San Diego were glad to see the Cup finally move to Auckland in 1995.

In sailing terms, there may not be a better venue than New Zealand to bring the Cup back to its former glory. Over the last decade, New Zealand has been one of the best-performing nations in many of the world's top sailing events. Through its boat-building, spar, and sail-making industries, it has developed a worldwide reputation and is recognized as being one of the best countries in the world to commission a high-performance yacht.

Indeed, there are high expectations that the 30th America's Cup may be regarded as the greatest sailing event ever. New Zealanders support their national sports teams with pride, and the America's Cup holds a special significance for many. The first challenge, in 1987, captured the imagination of many New Zealanders and presented the

very real possibility that this small country could in fact win such a prestigious prize. But no one could have predicted what would happen after Team New Zealand's victory in 1995. Four hundred thousand people crowded the streets in Auckland alone to congratulate the country and the team. It was one of the biggest outbursts of celebration New Zealand has ever had. It seemed almost everyone, and in some cases everything, including sheep, donned red socks and took to the streets in a huge outpouring of national pride.

Auckland, dubbed "the city of sails," is home to 1.3 million people, and 50,000 of them own a boat of some sort. When the 1993 Whitbread Round the World Race came to Auckland, 50,000 people were at the yacht harbor to greet the boats as they began arriving at 2:00 a.m. For the America's Cup series in 1999/2000, event organizers are expecting up to 200,000 people and over 5,000 spectator craft.

Like Fremantle, Auckland has developed a custom-built yacht harbor called the American Express New Zealand Cup Village. This will host all of the expected 13 foreign syndicates. But unlike any Cup before, the village will be centered in the heart of the city's waterfront. It is planned that the village will also provide facilities for some 60-plus "super yachts," including some of the magnificent J-class yachts.

The original Maori inhabitants viewed the Auckland region as a Garden of Eden because it was rich in bird and marine life. Today, while it still retains spectacular beaches and parks, the urban spread has grown to almost 50 miles in length. The region has over 48 dormant volcanic cones, and the America's Cup course area is flanked by one of the most dominant volcanic landmarks, Rangatoto Island. The weather in Auckland during January and February will be pleasantly warm for Cup competitors and visitors, averaging 75 degrees Fahrenheit.

The city has a cosmopolitan feel, with a large variety of top class cuisine and entertainment. The central focus is a new international casino in the Sky Tower, which is the tallest building in the Southern Hemisphere. This imposing structure provides a panoramic view of the various features in the area including the America's Cup harbor and course area.

Around the perimeter of the city are a number of exceptional vineyards. Some of the best are situated only a short distance from the course area on Waiheke Island.

Stonyridge Larose has been rated as one of the top twenty Cabernet blends in the world.

Besides Auckland, other parts of New Zealand are wonderful destinations for visitors. Dunedin, Christchurch, Queenstown, Wellington, Rotorua, the Bay of Islands, and the Coromandel Peninsula offer an incredible variety of activities and scenery. On the southern lakes and rivers one can fish for trout and salmon. In coastal areas such as the Bay of Islands or the appropriately named Bay of Plenty, fishing for marlin and swordfish is possible.

The wild side of New Zealand offers many challenges to those who seek excitement. Heli-skiing, bungee jumping, white- and black-water rafting, and paragliding are all available. For those who want to get closer to nature, several activities are alluring: swimming with the dolphins, whale-watching, or hiking in one of New Zealand's beautiful national parks. New Zealanders are proud that almost 25 percent of the country remains protected as natural land and bush.

Excitement is building for the people of Auckland and the rest of New Zealand. They are anxious to show the world the many natural treasures of this beautiful country. Winning yachting's most revered event is probably the nation's proudest accomplishment, and while there is little doubt the Kiwis will prove gracious hosts, they will also be rooting hard to defend the prized trophy during the 30th rendition of the regatta.

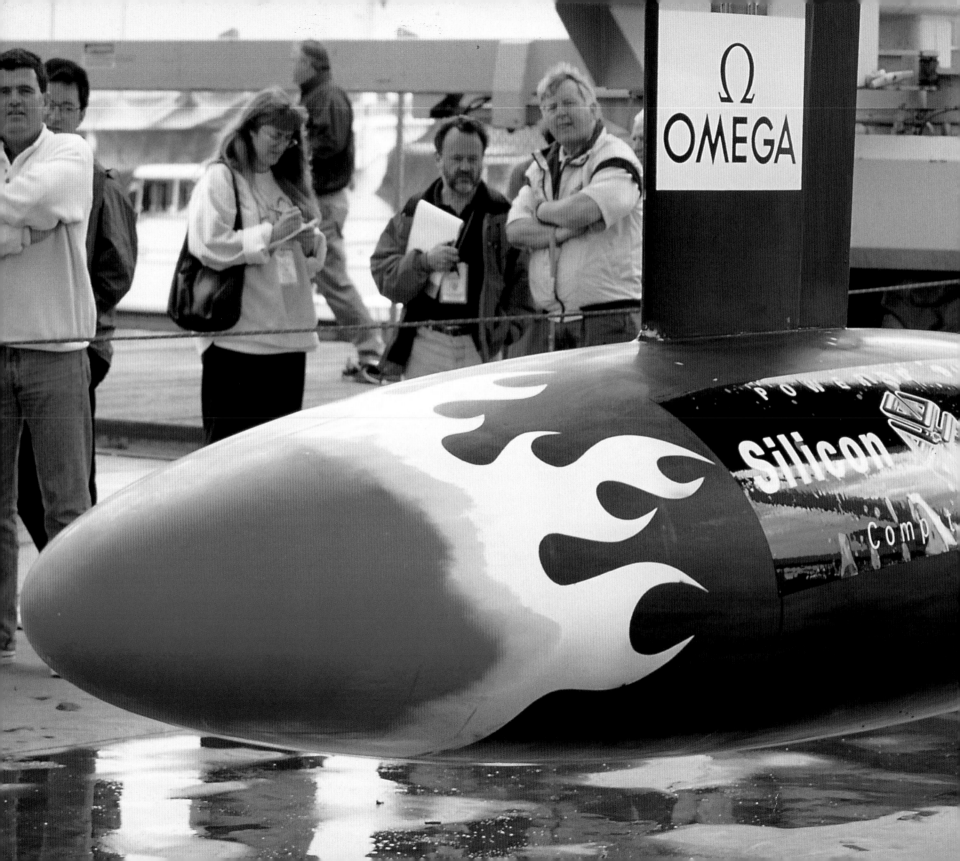

AMERICA'S CUP TECHNOLOGY

CHAPTER FOUR

AMERICA'S CUP TECHNOLOGY

Although the America's Cup is a sailboat race, it is also a high-powered design and technology contest. While the winner is determined on water, it is what happens on land that often separates the victor from the also-ran. History suggests that the fastest yacht wins, and the fastest yacht is usually the best design employing the most advanced technology.

It has been that way since the very first challenge, when the yacht *America* won the 100 Guinea Cup in 1851. In fact, the men responsible for building *America* did so in an effort to exhibit their nation's proficiency in the technical skills of boat design and boat building. The design was a breakthrough, and the yacht was by far the fastest on the 100 Guinea Cup course. This trend has been repeated throughout most of the America's Cup matches that have followed.

Some people believe that the modern regatta would be a fairer contest if it were sailed in identical yachts, so that the skill of the sailors would be the paramount factor in victory. Others counter that it is the secrecy, skill, complexity, and intrigue surrounding the design that gives the Cup its identity and makes it unique among sailing competitions.

Conceptually, today's America's Cup resembles Formula One motor racing. Like Formula One, it exploits highly sophisticated design, building, and advanced technology to produce the most refined racing yachts in the

Seventy-five years after the Revolutionary War, America's breakthrough design (seen in a replica at left) won the 1851 100 Guineas Cup against a fleet of British yachts. The 95-foot radical schooner, which demonstrated the superior American boat-building technology, had two steeply raked masts with no topsails and a single jib with no boom.

With an overall length of 144 feet and a mast height of 200 feet, Reliance was the largest boat ever to race for the America's Cup (the 16,600 square feet of sail could have equipped six contemporary Cup yachts). The awe-inspiring 1903 winner was also a product of Herreshoff's pioneering work with longitudinal construction.

world. While all designers and technicians must adhere to the same formula governing the type of yacht they can produce, they are still given a great deal of creative latitude in which to explore the speed frontier.

Although the racing yachts of today are considerably different from those of early America's Cup competitions, innovation has always been the hallmark of the event. Perhaps the most famous designer and builder in America's Cup history is the legendary American Nathanael Herreshoff. Remembered for his huge yachts that raced in five Cup regattas from 1893 to 1903, "Captain Nat" actually attracted more attention at the time with his succession of small catamarans that tore over the water's surface at speeds upwards of 20 miles per hour.

While the multihulls were certainly innovative, it was Herreshoff's creation of *Reliance* that probably stands as his most imaginative work. The largest boat ever to race for the America's Cup, the yacht serves as a clear example of the designer's concept of the exaggerated waterline through the use of extended overhangs forward and aft. The measured waterline length of *Reliance* was a little over 89 feet, but the length overall was close to 144 feet. The result was increased speed when the boat heeled as the overhangs translated into increased sailing length.

Herreshoff pushed the design and technology envelope by including a number of revolutionary additions to his boats. *Reliance* carried two steering wheels, a hollow rudder that could be filled with water or pumped dry to correct for weather helm, winches with ball bearings, and automatically shifting gears. Also on board were lightweight steel spars and a topmast that could be lowered into the mainmast for the purpose of saving weight aloft if the topmast was not being used.

As advanced as his design thinking was, it was actually Herreshoff's ideas on boat construction that many historians conclude was his true genius. First employed in building his 1901 Cup defender *Constitution*, the method of "longitudinal construction" was a web of steel frames that connected the keel, hull, and deck. The method pioneered by Herreshoff was used in both boat and airplane construction for the next half century.

One of Herreshoff's contemporaries was George Watson, the designer of Thomas Lipton's second *Shamrock*, which raced *Constitution*. The Irish boat was the first to be designed after models were towed in a test tank. This technological process has become a mainstay of America's Cup design ever since.

The 12-meter era, from 1958 to 1987, was witness to many technological, design, and boat-building advances. The first 12-meter defender, *Columbia*, exhibited the evolutionary reverse transom. The yacht was skippered by Briggs Cunningham, who invented the grommet in the mainsail named for him that is used for trim. The 1962 challenger *Gretel* was designed by the estimable Alan

Payne. He introduced coffee-grinder winches that added speed and efficiency to trimming the jib and tacking the boat. In 1967 the major innovation was the placement of almost all the winches below decks on the defender *Intrepid*. Below-deck winches had been used on both *Reliance* and *Enterprise* (1930), but not to such an extent or in the same configuration.

In 1974, *Courageous, Mariner,* and *Southern Cross* were the first 12-meter yachts to be built using aluminum, but they weren't the first to be built of that material in the America's Cup. That honor goes to *Defender* in 1895. In 1986, New Zealand's challenger was built using fiberglass. Since then exotic laminates such as carbon fiber have been used in hull and spar construction.

Historically, the use of technology has not been without its problems. Some syndicates employing the use of scale models found the results to be misleading. Britton Chance relied heavily on scale model results in designing the radical yacht *Mariner* for the 1974 defender trials. *Mariner* subsequently did not live up to expectations and left many designers questioning the validity of using such technology. However, during the same 12-meter era, designers such as Olin Stephens were employing similar technology to assist with the design of such great Cup yachts as *Intrepid*. Stephens, experimenting with different rudder positions and smoothing out the volume distribution aft, was able to correctly predict that the combined wave drag generated by the hull, keel, and rudder would be reduced.

By 1980, the first of the two-boat programs was being organized to test and refine various sails, keels, and hull changes. One boat was tested against another, and as an improvement was found, it would be used to leap-frog the performance of both yachts. Two-boat testing is an expensive and time-consuming method of refining a design. Although it is still used by the larger syndicates today, more confidence is being given to scale model testing.

The most controversial advance of the 12-meter era was the wing keel of *Australia II*, the 1983 challenger. The design itself was admirable, but there were unresolved suspicions that the Australian syndicate might have tested the keel in a towing tank in Holland, in violation of Cup rules. The keel, along with vertically cut upwind sails made of light and extremely durable Kevlar sailcloth, may have been the deciding factor in the storied contest. In the deciding race, on the final downwind leg, *Australia II* carried a smaller, more stable spinnaker to gain 1 minute and 18 seconds to pass the American defender *Liberty* and extract the America's Cup from the New York Yacht Club for the first time in history.

Determined to bring the Cup back home in 1987, Conner adopted the idea of a fully integrated design team. His people carried out extensive scientific testing, building three full-size test yachts. The final boat, *Stars & Stripes*, was longer and carried less sail than any of the opposition. In the strong winds off Fremantle, the yacht enjoyed a sig-

nificant speed edge to easily out perform the Australian defender, *Kookaburra III*, 4–0.

By 1992, Bill Koch had expanded the team concept to combine some of the top naval architects, marine scientists, and engineers in the U.S. He not only hired more scientific expertise than any previous America's Cup syndicate, he also elected to put a scientist rather than a yacht designer at the head of his design group. Though not a world-class sailor, Koch provided a new management style that focused on technology. He stipulated that the yacht should be fast enough so that even he would be able to helm it and win. The team produced *America³*, which defeated the Italian challenger, *Il Moro di Venezia*, 4–1.

In 1995, it was widely accepted that it would be very difficult to improve on Bill Koch's design effort. But on the other side of the world, New Zealand had assembled a formidable team that set out to challenge the level achieved by Koch. Many were surprised by the speed advantage that was subsequently attained. The New Zealand boat *Black Magic* became only the second non-American yacht to win the America's Cup, sweeping the defender 5–0. It was later observed that had *Black Magic*

The first yacht to defend the Cup at the Newport venue, Enterprise, is seen being launched from Herreshoff's boathouse (left) and at sail (right). The 1930 defender was designed by Starling Burgess with innovative below-deck winches (an approach that was further developed aboard the 1967 defender Intrepid). Much to Lipton's chagrin, Enterprise easily beat Shamrock V in the last stand for yachting's favorite Irishman.

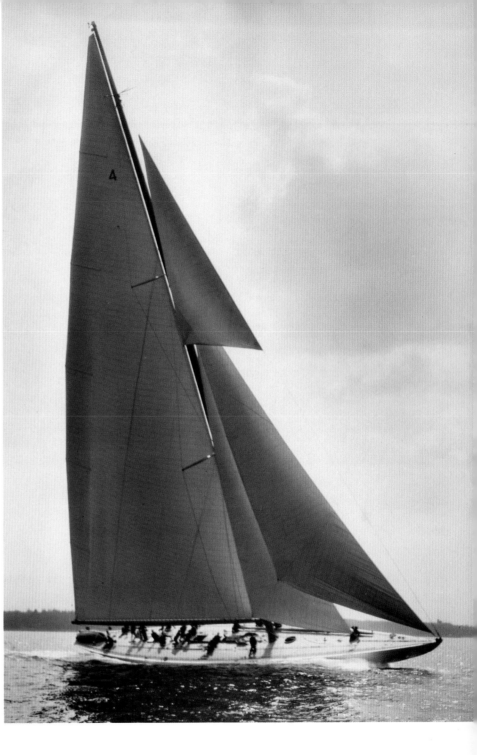

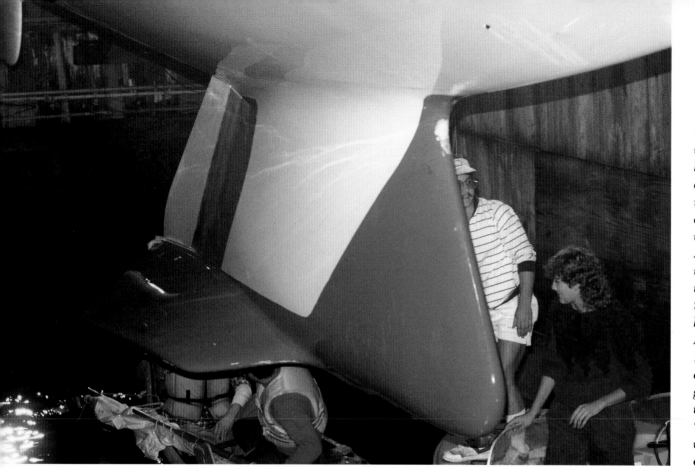

*Though unclear whether it was **Australia II**'s winged keel (left), its ultralight and durable sails or simply superior sailing which won the day in 1983, Dennis Conner was determined to avenge America's first defeat by taking an integrated approach to the design of **Stars & Stripes**, the boat with which he returned the Cup to American soil in 1987. In 1988, The New Zealanders' efforts to return to the elegant prewar J-boat era turned farcical when their "Big Boat" (right) was met with Conner's speedy, and easily victorious, catamaran.*

raced *America*[3], the New Zealand boat would have won by over five minutes!

All of the syndicates competing in the 1999/2000 Cup have adopted a scientific approach and structured themselves as large research programs. To make the breakthroughs that all Cup syndicates seek, today's yacht designer has a number of tools at his disposal which until recently didn't exist. Chief among these is the personal computer, which is being used for everything from drawing hull lines to analyzing competitors' shapes to acquiring real-time data while sailing. What used to be done by hand over a period of months as recently as the mid-1970s has

been reduced to a matter of hours as CAD-CAM (Computer Assisted Design-Computer Assisted Manufacturing) programs. These new efficiencies mean that more candidate designs can be considered over a shorter time span and at less cost. Developments in scale modeling, computer codes, engineering, aerodynamics, and hydrodynamics have given designers a better understanding of environmental forces, materials, construction techniques, and other factors that affect boat speed.

An advantage of only a few seconds can mean the difference between gaining the controlling position or being controlled. In predictable wind conditions, a difference of

a few seconds in boat speed rapidly increases to minutes over the length of the racecourse. No one feature looms as most important when it comes to maximizing speed: the hull, appendages, sails, and spars and their effects on one another are all key factors in producing a tiny increase in speed. It's no surprise that the America's Cup is often won or lost many months before the final race when key design decisions are made.

The technical teams preparing for New Zealand know that the designs that worked in the lighter conditions of San Diego won't necessarily translate to the more unpredictable, sometimes rugged wind and waves of Auckland. This will be

a major consideration when observing the three basic design parameters contained in the IACC rule: length (measured 250 mm above the waterline); sail area; and weight or displacement. The longer a yacht, the faster it will sail, particularly at high speeds when the yacht's own wake and waves become a large component of the overall drag. Additional sail area is always fast in light winds and when sailing downwind, except in very light winds or choppy seas where a big spinnaker may become unstable. In strong winds when sailing on an upwind leg, however, too much sail only increases the drag. In all yachts, there is a wind speed above which it is faster to reef, or reduce, sail area.

Increasing the weight of a yacht increases the amount of water that is displaced. In most cases, a heavier boat will sail slower than a lighter boat. However, in the case of an America's Cup boat, increasing the weight usually means increasing the lead on the bottom of the keel, called the bulb. The force provided by the bulb opposes the driving and overturning forces created by the sails, so a boat with a heavier bulb can utilize more driving force from the sails. IACC yachts will usually float longer when weight is added because the rule allows overhanging sterns and bows. Therefore, even if weight is added, making the boat displace more water, in certain conditions the additional length may provide less resistance. Accordingly, the rules restrict the amount of additional weight that can be carried.

In some important areas designers are allowed much more freedom. For example, the IACC rule contains no restrictions on stability. Teams are therefore encouraged to build their yachts as light as possible above the keel in order to gain as much stability as possible. This creates the huge engineering challenge of designing a yacht that is near the minimum strength required to withstand massive rigging loads, which can approach 25 tons. With no restriction on stability, all America's Cup boats use a very large bulb on the bottom of their keel to balance the huge overturning forces created by the sails and mast when sailing upwind. These bulbs typically weigh between 18,000 and 22,000 tons and are supported on a thin keel strut that is connected to the hull. It is not unusual for these keel struts to deflect more than four inches under sailing conditions.

The 1992 Cup was a race of millionaire syndicates. Bill Koch's reliance on technology (he made a scientist the head of his design team and demanded an all-out effort to increase boat speed) paid off when America[3] (near right) beat Raul Gardini's Il Moro di Venezia *(far right).*

The IACC rule imposes an upper limit on beam of 5.5 meters, but there is no lower limit, so designers must decide how narrow to build their boats for maximum advantage. Reducing beam reduces wetted surface, until the yacht becomes almost spherical in cross section. However, reducing beam also reduces stability, and designers will therefore have to relate beam to the optimum wind strength they have chosen. A wider boat may be faster upwind in stronger winds, but the trade-off is that it might be slower downwind.

The America's Cup rule on hull shape is relatively open, although there can be no hollows, and there is a limit on girth at the forward and aft waterline stations. For the most part, designers are free to choose their fastest shape within their chosen length and beam.

Defining the optimum yacht design will be especially tricky for the competition in 1999/2000 because Auckland presents the most varied conditions of any venue in America's Cup history. Wind speeds could vary between eight and 30 knots, possibly all within the span of a single race. Wave conditions are likely to be relatively smooth in a southerly wind direction and yet very rough when the wind swings to the northerly quadrant. Depending on the decision made to optimize for smooth or rough water, designing for sea conditions may require a totally

The personal computer (left) has revolutionized America's Cup technology. New tools, such as CAD-CAM (Computer Assisted Design-Computer Assisted Manufacturing) programs and VPPs (Velocity Prediction Programs), have reduced a yacht designer's work in some cases from months to a matter of hours. A towing tank (below) is also extremely useful for isolating and validating factors used in VPP tests.

different treatment for detailing the forward sections of the hull.

In southerly wind conditions, wind shifts and oscillations in a breeze ranging between 10 and 30 degrees will not be uncommon, and the yachts will need to do more tacking and maneuvering. These conflicting natural conditions will no doubt promote a lot of thought and discussion pertaining to the choices of length, beam, bow shape, sail area, weight, and structural stiffness required for the "ideal" yacht to race in 2000.

Teams rely on a wide variety of tools to help them orchestrate the many choices, but having the right personnel is critical. Syndicates generally invest heavily in seasoned designers, scientists, and engineers whose previous experience reduces the amount of testing required to produce a superior yacht. The fact of the matter is that when a design choice cannot be validated scientifically, intuition and experience are vital.

A combination of methods and techniques is used to cross-check and confirm test results and design decisions. These may include several VPPs (velocity prediction programs), a water tunnel or towing tank, a wind tunnel, engineering programs such as FE (finite element) studies, sail programs, and CFD codes (computational fluid dynamics).

The VPP, the most widely used design tool, balances the sail forces (lift and drag) with the lift and drag of the hull and appendages at various wind speeds and sailing angles. A VPP gives designers the ability to estimate the optimum speeds of a design candidate in a given wind or sea condition. To output its prediction, the VPP utilizes most of the factors relating to speed, including length, beam, hull stiffness, hull shape, stability, wetted surface area, sail area, rig windage, and crew weight.

A wind tunnel is valuable mainly for appendage work and sail measurements. High-speed tunnels can generate the same conditions for the candidate model as experienced in the full size version. *America³* used half-scale models in 1992, and Team New Zealand used quarter-scale models in 1995. Most agree that models less than one-ninth scale are too small to achieve the required accuracy. The wind tunnel was also used in 1995 by Team New Zealand to measure sail forces on one-ninth scale models to refine concepts concerning sail shape and size. This exercise reduced the need for full size sail testing and increased the practical limit for the design matrix, with over 120 spinnaker models being tested.

The differences in candidate hulls and appendages are measured in a towing tank. Scale models are towed from a carriageway down a large pool (often 300m in length). The forces are measured, scaled to full size, averaged, and corrected before the data is applied to a VPP where the hull forces are combined with the sail forces. The towing tank is also used to isolate and validate various features that are incorporated into a VPP.

Even though the appendages are attached below the water surface, they are still close enough to contribute to the surface waves. The pressure and lift forces on a yacht's hull and keel combine to produce a complex series of waves and wave troughs, the extent of which provides a significant component of the overall drag.

By the time the challengers arrive in Auckland, they will have thoroughly simulated and tested New Zealand's unpredictable wind and wave conditions. In strong winds, America's Cup hulls and keels can combine to produce large wave troughs, which can be a significant component of the total hull drag (left). Using a wind tunnel (right), Team New Zealand was able to measure sail forces on one-ninth scale models to refine concepts concerning sail shape and size. This reduced the need for full-size sail testing and increased the practical limit of the design matrix, with over 120 spinnaker models being tested.

One tool that teams employ as sparingly as possible is full-size testing, which is very expensive and slow. Moreover, because it is carried out in a natural environment, with its constantly changing weather conditions, it is often difficult to isolate individual components or make meaningful comparisons between tests, which cannot, given their setting, be carried out under identical circumstances.

How well a team interprets the data gathered in its prodigious research program—and transforms it into a state-of-the-art speed machine ideally suited to Auckland—will very possibly determine where the America's Cup trophy resides after March 2000. Happily, the win-

ning boat won't necessarily have been bought for top dollar. Team New Zealand's 1995 campaign reportedly came in for less than $15 million, far less than the $70 million it cost *America³* to win in 1992.

The Kiwis also proved that a small country of only 3.5 million people could compete with far larger and richer nations and push America's Cup technology to a new level. And not to be forgotten is the skill of the sailors who harnessed their boat's potential and deployed it strategically and tactically. The same combination of technology and sailing expertise will be needed to win in 2000 and the team that best joins the two will lift the Cup in victory.

CHAPTER FIVE

RACING ONE ON ONE

RACING ONE ON ONE

Tactically, the modern America's Cup is a different kind of race from most sailing regattas. The majority are fleet races in which a number of boats compete against each other. This was actually the format of the 1851 race that led to the establishment of the America's Cup when the yacht *America* took on 15 British vessels in the 100 Guinea Cup. The original Deed of Gift, the document written in 1857 that outlined the rules for the America's Cup regatta, stated that "any organized yacht club of any foreign country shall always be entitled…to claim the right of sailing a match for this cup…."

The exact definition of the word "match" has led to a number of disagreements over the years, but it has come to define the format of the modern America's Cup. In fact, match racing, in which one boat races another, has been the style of competition in this regatta since 1871. The first America's Cup regatta was actually in 1870, but 18 New York Yacht Club schooners were entered versus *Cambria* from Great Britain. And purists might not agree that the 1871 event was a true match race, since the NYYC assigned four different yachts to race against *Livonia*, although each race was a one-on-one affair.

For spectators, a match race is easy to understand because it's simple to determine which of the two boats is leading. For skippers and crew, match racing is a little more complicated as it demands substantially different strategies and techniques from those on board. Tactics are different from those employed in a fleet race and often mean the difference between winning and losing. If two yachts focus only on each other in a fleet race, they will

Pre-start action during the 1995 Cup featured **NZL-39** *with Chris Dickson helming and performing a jibe reversal to gain starboard advantage on* **Nippon,** *still on port.*

In this photo taken during the 1995 America's Cup, both **Black Magic** *(left) and* **Young America** *are on starboard tack and overlapped.* **Young America** *is the leeward boat and thus* **Black Magic** *must keep clear. As the two boats approach the mark,* **Young America** *is the inside boat and must be given room to round the mark.*

lose too much distance relative to the other yachts. Beating the single opponent is all that matters in match racing.

Position on the course relative to the other boat becomes a key factor. It is not necessary to sail around the course as fast as possible, which is the case in most fleet and handicap races. In many cases, sailing extra distances in order to control a position or force the opponent farther behind offers the greater advantage. The strategy for

match racing has been loosely described as "trying to figure out where the opponent wants to be and then getting in the way."

Because the America's Cup is not a regularly calendar event—it depends on the scheduling vagaries of the defender—the match-racing format, with its unique strategies and tactics, was not widely practiced until the early 1980s. At that time, a circuit of match-racing events began to develop worldwide allowing skippers, crews, and umpires to test and refine their skills. Today, over 1,200 international teams are ranked, and hundreds of match-race regattas are held each year. Most of the skippers and crews that will compete in the 1999/2000 America's Cup

THE TWO BASIC RULES OF SAILING

PORT AND STARBOARD
Near right: When sailing into the wind, if two yachts approach each other on opposite tacks, the boat on the right, Red, is on starboard. The boat on the left, Green, is on port and must give way.

WINDWARD KEEPS CLEAR OF LEEWARD
Far right: Under the rules, Red may luff Green because Red is leeward or downwind of Green. For this rule to apply, both yachts must be on the same tack.

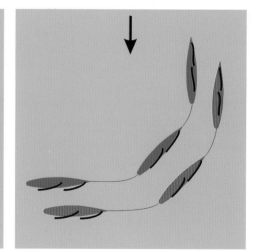

*Both **USA-36** and **NZL-32** are on starboard tack (left) with NZL-32 moving into leeward, and right of way, position.*

During the 1992 America's Cup, Il Moro (red boat) is the leeward boat and has control over America[3]. In this photo (right), Paul Cayard at the helm of Il Moro is in the process of luffing up Buddy Melges in America[3]. In a moment, the two asymmetrical spinnakers will collapse.

races have been regular competitors on the match-racing circuit, and the sport is constantly changing as crews continually experiment and adopt new techniques in an effort to outsmart their opponents.

In the challenger trials that begin in Auckland in October 1999, the match-racing format will be used. Each of the challengers will compete in four round-robin series that will lead to a semifinal series and then to a final

match of two challenger yachts. The winner will then face Team New Zealand, the America's Cup defender by right of its 1995 victory in San Diego. That match will consist of up to nine races, the winner being the first yacht to record five wins.

Let's now consider some of the key tactics and strategies that spectators and television viewers will observe during the racing.

Tactically, the start involves aggressive use of the rules and practiced offensive and defensive strategies. Crews will employ a philosophy similar to a fighter pilot trying to win a dogfight against an enemy aircraft. They will use the rules to jostle, maneuver, and establish position. Winning the start can be the deciding factor in 70 percent of all match races.

Yachts are required to enter the starting area from opposite ends of the starting line five minutes before the starting signal. One yacht enters from the starboard side (right side looking toward the first mark) and the other enters from the port side. If either yacht fails to enter the pre-start area within two minutes, it will be penalized. This rule is designed to encourage the boats to meet and engage in pre-start maneuvering at least three minutes prior to the start of the race.

For a helmsman, the start is undoubtedly one of the tensest situations during the entire race. Both yachts, each weighing as much as 25 tons, converge on each other on a collision course. In the stronger winds expected in Auckland, this situation will test the reactions and nerves of even the very best helmsmen and crews. In strong winds, these big America's Cup yachts of more than 75 feet are overpowered and extremely difficult to handle. Originally designed for San Diego conditions averaging 10 knots, they will face a different proposition in Auckland, where they may race in 25 knots of wind.

Because each yacht carries its own momentum, there is a slight delay when either yacht maneuvers, reacting to a particular situation. A starboard tack yacht has full rights over a port tack yacht. However, the starboard tack yacht cannot do a late turn (or alteration of course) if as a result of the turn the port tack yacht is then

*As **USA-36** and **NZL-32** head upwind at the start of a 1995 Cup race, the Americans are in front, but the New Zealanders are actually in a better position as they are upwind and thus closer to the windward mark.*

unable to keep clear. Therefore, in the entry situation, a port tack yacht will often avoid a starboard tacker early enough to be able to stay clear of the starboard tacker but late enough that the distance between the yachts is so small that the starboard tacker is restricted from altering its course. Performed correctly, the port tack yacht will escape the control of a starboard tacker.

Precision is key here. If the port tack yacht leaves its turn too late, it will foul the starboard tacker. If it turns

During pre-start maneuvers, NZL-32 and AUS-31 approach each other on opposite tacks, each guarding against the other from gaining the controlling position astern of their yacht. As soon as one of the yachts turns to attempt to get astern of the opponent, the other yacht will do the same, thus beginning circling tactics often seen in match races.

and avoids too early, the starboard tack yacht will be able to match the turn and force the port tacker completely onto starboard in a controlled position. In forcing an opponent to tack, the controlling yacht can effectively

LIMITATION ON STARBOARD ALTERING COURSE

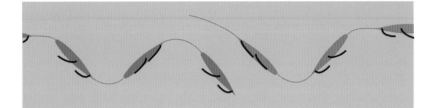

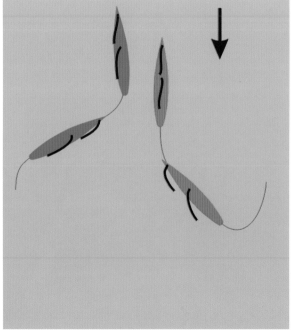

Above: Green on port tack (wind coming over the left side of the boat) tries to keep clear of Red on starboard. Red must give Green an option to escape. Once the boats get very close, Red cannot alter course unless Green is able to react and still keep clear. In this case, Red cannot alter course and Green has escaped the control of Red. The key question umpires ask is whether Green was able to keep clear.

Right: Green on port turns to avoid Red on starboard. If Green turns too early, Red will have enough space to turn and aim at Green. Green will again have to keep clear in this case, being forced to tack. Red now controls the right side of the pre-start.

Pre-start circling is illustrated here (left). Whichever boat is able to circle or turn faster will eventually gain controlling position.

block the right-hand side of the starting line, thereby always retaining starboard tack rights and limiting the options of the opponent.

When yachts are on the same tack, much of the early pre-start advantage is gained by establishing a position astern of the opponent. A following yacht can effectively prevent a yacht in front from turning because a yacht that is changing tacks (turning) has no rights under the rules. Hence a trailing yacht can force an opponent to

sail away from the favorable position. The yacht trapped ahead will weave and slow down, attempting to shake a trailing yacht off its stern.

To guard against this situation, when both yachts first engage they will often circle each other (see photo on page 99). When initially circling, neither boat has control over the other. However, if one boat is able to circle or turn slightly faster than the other, it will eventually gain the controlling position behind. (see photo on page 100). When one yacht begins to lose position, a classic countermove is to head for the

CONTROLLING FROM ASTERN

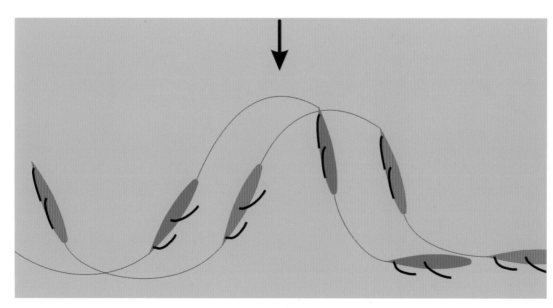

Red can match any course change by Green. Under the rules, Green cannot tack or jibe without fouling Red for two reasons. The rules say Green cannot tack or jibe in Green's water. Also, if Green did tack or jibe, it would become a port tack yacht that has to give way to Red. Red is therefore controlling Green.

spectator fleet. Once among the spectator boats, the lead boat can circle around a spectator vessel without the trailing boat being able to cut inside and block the turn.

On the final approach to the starting line, calculating the distance to the starting line versus the time remaining is the key question. Ideally the yacht will cross the line just after the starting signal. Judging the approach is made more demanding by the changing wind conditions: The boat accelerates, decelerates, and changes direction as the wind gusts affect its performance. With 25 tons of momentum, a yacht reaching the line too early may find

SITUATIONS AT THE STARTING LINE

THE POWER OF A CIRCLING ADVANTAGE
Clockwise from top of diagram: Red, having gained in the circles, tacks close astern of Green. Green must jibe in order to prevent Red setting up in a position close behind. As Green jibes, Red is able to build speed, separating to the right side of Green.

CIRCLING CONTINUED
Red now has created enough room to jibe and aim at Green. Green, on port, is forced to tack and Red now controls the right side of the pre-start.

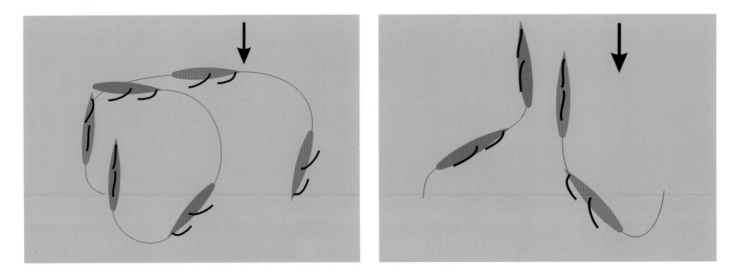

it difficult to slow down enough not to cross early and yet still achieve maximum speed at the starting signal. On the other hand, neither yacht wants to be late!

Navigators use computers and GPS (Global Positioning System) equipment, which pinpoints positions using satellites to help predict the time required to reach the starting line.

EFFECTS OF A STARTING LINE BIAS

If the wind is not perpendicular to the starting line, it will favor one boat. In this case, the wind has veered to the right favoring the Red boat, even if Green crosses the starting line first.

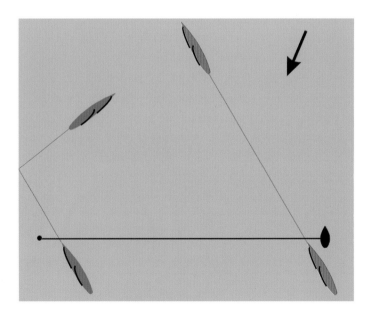

This photo illustrates the classic tactic of shaking off the controlling yacht astern by using a spectator vessel. The lead boat can circle around the vessel without the trailing boat being able to cut inside and block the turn.

THE FIRST (UPWIND) LEG

After the start, the yachts will race into the wind toward a mark that is 3.275 nautical miles away. This leg is often referred to as the first beat. The wind and currents are never constant and will shift during the leg favoring a certain track. On the course area in Auckland the current can be as strong as 2 knots and the wind could shift between 10 and 40 degrees during a single upwind leg. This puts the pressure on the tactician, who is responsible for reading the wind and currents, as well as for predicting what the opponent will do and when he will do it. The tactician then relays that information to the helmsman.

If either boat has gained an advantage at the start, it can choose the favored tack and will often force the opponent onto the less-favored course. "Covering" an opponent is one of the most common tactics in match racing. Simply stated, covering refers to the situation in which the leading boat is positioned such that the disturbed wind from its own sails falls onto the opponent's yacht. The trailing yacht is forced to tack in the opposite direction to escape the disturbed wind. Not only does the disturbed wind affect the yacht's performance, but the additional tack also results in a loss of speed and distance.

A "tight cover" is when a lead boat matches a trailing boat tack for tack, blanketing the wind continuously. The lead crew will usually adopt this tactic if they feel they have an advantage tacking. The trailing yacht may try everything to break such a cover, including "false tacks." This is the term used when the yacht gives every appearance that it is going through a tack but actually performs only half the tack and then returns to the original course. The objective is to trick the opponent into going through with the complete tack, thus gaining "clear air" as the two yachts continue in different directions. The fitness and power of the crew are measured by their performance in the tacks as they furiously work to overcome the power of the sails and outlast the opposition crew. A tacking duel adds greater meaning to the phrase "survival of the fittest!"

The red boat on starboard tack has rights over the white boat on port tack. The umpires follow close behind to observe any alterations of course and rule infractions.

In race four of the 1987 America's Cup challenger series, New Zealand's *KZ-7* with Chris Dickson at the helm tacked over 100 times, tight covering *Stars & Stripes,* skippered by Dennis Conner. Although *Stars & Stripes* was the faster boat, *KZ-7* won that race principally because of employing the covering tactic. However, the crew's tactics were not as successful in the other races, and *KZ-7* lost the series 4–1. Conner and *Stars & Stripes* went on to easily beat Australia's *Kookaburra III* in the Cup match and return to the United States with the trophy.

Choosing the correct tack after the start is often predetermined by weather forecasts or a current difference that favors one side of the course. However, the skill of the tactician to read the wind on the water is vital. To the trained eye, the appearance of the water's surface indicates the strength and direction of the approaching wind and can indicate the optimum course, much the same as plotting a route using a road map. Occasionally, yachts will send a crew member up the mast to get a better view of the changing conditions. Navigators also record the wind history and current strength on computers, which can help predict likely wind and current effects.

Starting with the correct sail combination is also a key factor to success. Sails are designed to have an optimum depth for a particular wind and sea condition. If these conditions change, the crews will consider changing sails during the leg. Time may be lost while the sail is changed, and the yacht will be forced to hold its course while the replacement sail is being prepared. Tacticians will balance the gain in performance after a sail change is made versus

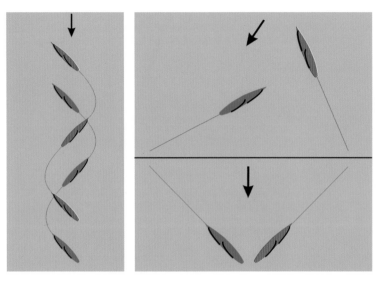

UPWIND SITUATIONS

TIGHT COVERING
Left: Red is tight covering Green. Green will be feeling disturbed wind from Red's influence and will be losing speed.
THE EFFECT OF WINDSHIFTS
Right: Red and Green are initially even but on opposite tacks. The wind veers right meaning the boat on the right will gain.

the positional losses that may occur during the change.

There is almost always an opportunity to make gains at the first rounding mark. Tacticians and navigators work hard to establish the correct line on which to approach or "lay" the mark, called the "layline." Of course, in shifting conditions, this approach is constantly changing. If the layline is judged incorrectly, the yacht

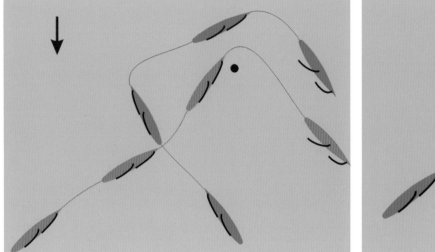

THE TOP MARK

THE DECISION TO APPROACH ON PORT OR STARBOARD
Left: Red on port dips Green's stern very close.
Green is forced to sail past Red, because under the rules,
Green cannot tack in Red's water. Green therefore sails
extra distance, past the layline, and loses the lead.

Right: Green cannot dip Red and still lay the mark. Red
must give way to Green because Red is on starboard
tack. Red retains the lead.

may be forced to perform two extra tacks, slowing its progress considerably. A slight loss in speed at this point in the race can be very expensive because after rounding the mark, the crew will then hoist the spinnaker, and that initially results in a further speed loss. Once a 25-ton yacht is slowed, it can take over 45 seconds to accelerate back to the previous speed.

In the America's Cup, all rounding marks are rounded to starboard (or clockwise). The trailing yacht can be positioned to force the leading yacht to perform an extra tack to protect its starboard tack rights. The yacht ahead will still hold the lead, but it will have lost some distance and perhaps the controlling position for the following downwind leg.

On the downwind leg, called the run, the trailing boat has the opportunity to attack. Two of the most famous America's Cup races ever sailed are graphic examples of this. In the final and determining seventh race in 1983, *Australia II* overcame a 49-second lead by Dennis Conner on the last leg to become the first-ever non-American yacht to win the America's Cup in its then 132-year history. But an even more spectacular comeback occurred in 1995 when Conner gained a remarkable 4 minutes plus on the final downwind leg to catch the crew of *Mighty Mary* in the deciding race of the defender trials. The victory sent the well-known American skipper and his world-class crew into the Cup match against Team New Zealand, where they were unable to overcome the speed of the Kiwi yacht called *Black Magic.*

The downwind leg is often payback time for the trailing yacht. When sailing downwind, if the yacht behind is close enough to the opponent to block the wind, it can control or influence the course sailed by both yachts. If a yacht can gain an advantage by sailing into stronger winds, the gains downwind are much greater and last longer because the boats are moving at almost the same speed as the wind.

After rounding the top or windward mark, the decision of which course to choose for the run is therefore critical. Yachts will choose either a bear-away set on port tack or perform a gibe set onto starboard tack. A gibe set is a slower maneuver by about half a boat length, but if it results in a position on the course that provides the most favorable breeze, then it often is the best option.

If upwind sail choice is important, on downwind legs it is absolutely paramount. The rule allows for either of two different types of downwind spinnakers to be set. One is a symmetrical spinnaker that is set in stronger winds. Alternatively an asymmetrical spinnaker, or gennaker, can be used. While a gennaker is faster in lighter winds than a symmetrical sail, it is also more difficult to gibe. A bad

Both yachts are on starboard tack with the boat on the right unable to jibe onto port tack. The boat on the left is said to retain the starboard tack advantage. However, the boat on the right has the possibility of gaining inside room rights at the leeward mark.

gennaker gibe can be a race loser, and this fact is always a consideration when choosing between the two sails.

Two positioning options are always debated by the tacticians and strategists as the yachts approach the bottom rounding mark. One is to protect the starboard tack, and the other is to protect the inside position at the mark. The problem is that these two options are in conflict with each other. To retain starboard tack you must stay to the left of an opponent. To gain inside rights you must stay to the right.

Inside rights come into force only when the yachts are

DOWNWIND SITUATIONS

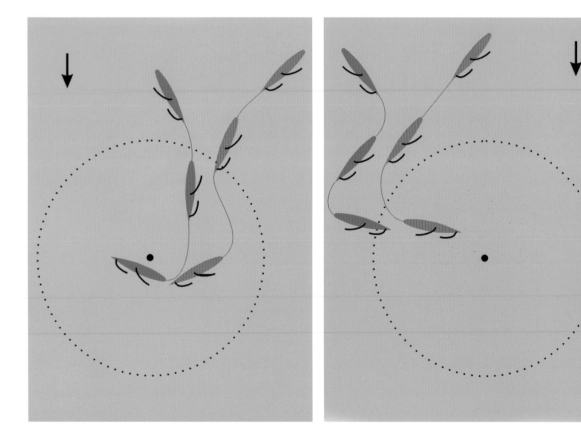

ROOM AT LEEWARD MARK
Far left: Red, on starboard, must give Green, on port, room to round the mark because Green is on the inside when it reaches the two-boat-length circle. In this case, rights to room override the rights of starboard tack.

Left: Red as starboard tack boat has rights over Green. Green cannot ask for room to round the leeward mark as it is not inside the imaginary two-boat-length circle. Starboard tack rights override room rights at this point. Red can therefore force Green to sail past the mark and then jibe to lead Green around. Had Green been able to stay alongside Red after the boats had jibed, Green would have become the inside boat with the right to ask for room.

within two boat lengths of the rounding mark. Until that point the boats are governed by the basic racing rules such as port and starboard. However, the advantage of securing the inside position may come into effect much farther up the leg. Sometimes yachts will gibe set at the

Green must give Red room to round the mark, but after Red has rounded, the effect of the "room" rule no longer applies. Green may luff and Red must keep clear. This is a useful move by Green if the left side of the course is favored, because Green has forced Red to the right.

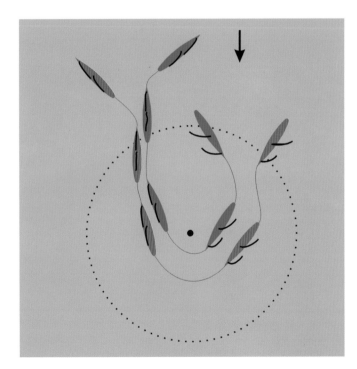

top mark in order to protect inside rights three miles away at the bottom mark! Such tactics employed so far in advance have led observers to comment that match racing is like playing chess. Positioning is critical in both endeavors. In match racing, it is often the case that you will be ultimately either rewarded or punished for a decision made 20 minutes earlier during a downwind leg.

The rules for all parts of the race are enforced by on the water judges and umpires. Prior to 1987, yachts used to protest each other for any perceived infringement and then spend hours after a race debating their case in front of a jury. It was not uncommon for the final result to be posted the following day! The penalty was almost always disqualification, which was a harsh penalty for what was often a minor breach of a rule. Now most of the rule decisions are instantaneous, and although a penalty will cost a yacht approximately six boat lengths in lost distance, the race is not over. The penalized yacht, although at a disadvantage, can still come back to win the race.

On an upwind leg, the penalty is a gibe. On the downwind leg, a penalized yacht must first lower its spinnaker and then perform a tack before continuing to race.

Some of the more aggressive match-racing skippers have developed moves that may trap an opponent into committing a penalty. Look for these moves during the pre-start maneuvering and at the rounding marks. If the boats are similar in speed, the difference between winning and losing in the challenger trials and the 2000 America's Cup may be how well a team knows and executes the strategies and tactics of match racing.

FOR THE DEFENSE: TEAM NEW ZEALAND

CHAPTER SIX

FOR THE DEFENSE:
TEAM NEW ZEALAND

Most America's Cup competitors and observers agree that Team New Zealand's dominating performance in 1995 brought the game to a new level. It is estimated by comparing times around the course in similar conditions that *Black Magic* would have beaten the '92 winner, *America³*, by over six minutes. Given the Kiwis' relatively small budget of $15 million, a population of only 3.5 million people, and seemingly less technological sophistication than the larger countries competing, the victory is all the more impressive.

Team New Zealand's goal has been to train at least two complete crews capable of winning the America's Cup. This has resulted in a higher standard of internal competition, ensuring highly qualified backups for all crew positions. Since 1995, there have at times been as many as four TNZ teams competing around the world in match-racing events.

Defending the Cup in 2000 represents a different proposition than winning it for the first time. Before *Australia II*'s victory in 1983, the Americans had successfully defended the Cup for 132 years. Since 1983, however, the Cup has been won by the challengers three times but successfully defended only twice—the big boat/catamaran mismatch in 1988 and *America³*'s victory in 1992. America is the only nation ever to successfully defend the Cup. The swing in advantage is due in part to changes in the rules that allow more widespread use of technology, as well as the sheer number of challengers as compared to the defender. For 2000, 12 challengers will compete, while Team New Zealand is the lone defender. The odds may favor the challenging group, which will have the advantage of a wider spread of ideas and the benefit of being able to race each other and gauge respective performance. On February 19, 2000, TNZ will line up against the best chal-

*Coutts (right), who skippered **Black Magic** to its 1995 victory, will be behind the wheel again in 2000. The challenger who wins the Louis Vuitton Cup and the right to sail against TNZ (left) may by then have raced a formidable 70 races or more in the course of the five-month trials. TNZ knows that their challenger will be in fighting prime.*

lenger and will only then be able to gauge its performance versus the rest of the world. Defending the Cup may well prove to be more difficult than winning it.

Whatever the sport, there is a danger that a team or an individual trying to retain a title approaches that challenge by being overly defensive and conservative in preparation and execution. To avoid that trap, Team New Zealand members may be better served believing they are trying to win the Cup rather than defending it!

Much of the successful team from 1995 has been retained. On the surface, retaining the same knowledge and skill from last time should be an advantage. However, if 1995 represented the best ideas the team had, developing new ideas may be more difficult. One of the challenges TNZ faces after the success of 1995 is to bring the game to yet another new level. The performance achieved last time will not be adequate five years later. Advances in technology, thinking, and management should mean the new America's Cup is contested at an even higher level.

When one of the experienced members of the Australian defense for 1987 was asked about their failure, he responded, "Complacency was one of the key reasons we lost." The team was not chasing new ideas and improvement with the same passion, and new team members did

not receive the same stature as those that were involved in 1983. The old ways prevailed, and although they were good enough in 1983, better thinking in 1987 eclipsed them.

After such a dominant performance in 1995, complacency may once again be one of the biggest threats to a successful defense of the Cup in 2000. The team has also matured in the five-year gap, and personal goals may have changed. The individual roles will have to reflect these changes.

Peter Blake and Alan Sefton once again reprise the roles

Simon Daubney (far left), Craig Monk, and Dean Phipps (without cap, front foreground) train for 2000. In Fremantle, victor Dennis Conner used his strongest crew members when the winds were high, and TNZ is expected to adopt the same tactic, stacking its race boat with bigger and stronger sailors for conditions of 20 knots or more.

of management and fund raising that they so capably played in 1995. Skipper Russell Coutts is back as head of the sailing team, and Tom Schnackenberg once again is supervising the design and technology teams.

How then, has TNZ changed since 1995? One of the most significant changes is that Doug Peterson and David Egan moved to the Italian camp, joining the Prada-sponsored syndicate. In what seems like a similar strategy to TNZ's 1995 effort, the Italians moved to secure Peterson at an early stage to start the technology race in a similar position to the defenders. TNZ replaced Peterson with Clay Oliver, who was involved with Dennis Conner's Stars & Stripes syndicate in their successful 1987 win. Oliver also played a pivotal role in TNZ's 1995 victory as he designed the VPP (Velocity Prediction Program) to measure performance. Oliver is believed to have improved the accuracy of the VPP and to have contributed new ideas for hull design.

One of TNZ's key focuses has been to improve the understanding of the effects of certain components in the 1995 design. The results of those efforts should lead to refining the overall design or perhaps, as rumored, lead to experimental concepts. Having access to Clay Oliver full time will no doubt improve the level of scientific knowl-

edge within the group. Nick Holroyd was also hired to assist with performance prediction and run the various CFD codes that the team is now using.

Over the past three summers that the team has been testing full-size yachts in Waitemata Harbor, Mike Drummond has played a dominant role in managing the on-the-water test program. In fact, most of the design team have played an active role on the water, a technique used to great success in the 1995 campaign. This gives the designers and technical people a firsthand understanding of the test results and increases communication between the sailing and design teams. Again the focus has been on rationalizing the reasons behind the various differences in performance to allow more accuracy in the final design. One of the more important features tested included the precise relationship between sail area versus waterline length related to the America's Cup rule. As sail area is reduced, waterline length can be increased, which will produce a boat that will be better in stronger winds. The amount of sail area selected will prove to be a key point in configuring the defending yacht against what the team perceives to be the performance of the best challenging yacht.

Another key feature tested was bow shapes. During 1997, the meter bow of *NZL 38* was replaced with a destroyer-type bow to test the effect in the different sea conditions of Auckland. The previous year, *NZL 38* had her mast position moved forward to test the effects of balance with less angle on the rudder in stronger winds.

Material and structural testing has also been a big factor in Team New Zealand's testing. The windier conditions

During team training exercises and boat-speed testing, Murray Jones (above) was usually at the helm of one of the black boats with Coutts or Dean Baker at the other. A skilled helmsman, Jones is considered Coutts' viable backup for the 2000 race. Chris Ward (opposite) is another member of the determined TNZ clan.

have meant a significant shift in mindset from San Diego where yachts competed in almost all races in under 20 knots of wind. Measuring the precise loads on rigging should mean that the final yacht can be built close to the minimum weight possible without risking failure.

In San Diego, TNZ's weather program was widely regarded as one of the major strengths of the tactical team. Bob Rice and Mike Drummond worked with uncanny accuracy to determine which side of the course would be favored on the first leg. The sailing team became supremely confident of their predictions and began to rely on their decisions without question. Auckland's shifting conditions may make this part of the program even more vital. Peter Evans, who was a tactician for Nippon Challenge in 1995 and has also won the match racing worlds as a tactician with Coutts, was hired to work with Rice. Having sailed almost his entire career on the waters of the racecourse, Evans brings a fundamental knowledge of the racing area. He has won two Olympic trials in the same waters and is reported to have brought the weather program to a new level.

The sailing team has been boosted in numbers, with eight new sailors joining the team. Only two sailors moved to competing camps after 1995. Coutts and the team were quick to seize this opportunity to bring in new talent. Grant Loretz was hired almost immediately to assist with the sail program, and Barry MacKay was moved into the sailing program. Former kayak specialist John MacBeth, after being tested and trained as a grinder for 12 months, was also given a full-time role.

Loretz crewed on Chris Dickson's America's Cup contender *Tag Heuer* in 1995 and was with New Zealand Challenge in 1992 as a primary sail trimmer. He is a skilled and respected sail designer and brings a wealth of experience together with some new thinking to the sail program. MacKay was also involved in New Zealand's 1992 effort. He was brought into the boat-building program late in 1995 after crewing with Peter Blake on the 90-foot catamaran *ENZA*, in their successful Jules Verne Round The World record attempt.

Realizing they will not enjoy the same variety of competition that the challengers will during the Louis Vuitton Cup, the team has set about increasing the level of skill throughout their group. The aim is to produce at least two equal crews, each capable of winning the America's Cup. The result will be a better standard of internal competition and suitable backups for all crew positions. At times there have been at least four TNZ teams competing around the world in match-racing events as well as ocean races, IMS Maxis, 50 footers, world championships, and Admirals Cups.

One of the features of the current team is the amount of depth and experience. In 1996 Coutts and his Team Magic crew had one of their most successful years ever, dominating every Brut Sailing Series event and the world championship. They have since been unable to repeat that form, although they have not been regular attendees on the match-racing circuit, choosing to concentrate on other events. But during 1997 and 1998, Team Magic never finished below the top two positions in events that they entered. It should also be noted that Coutts, together with

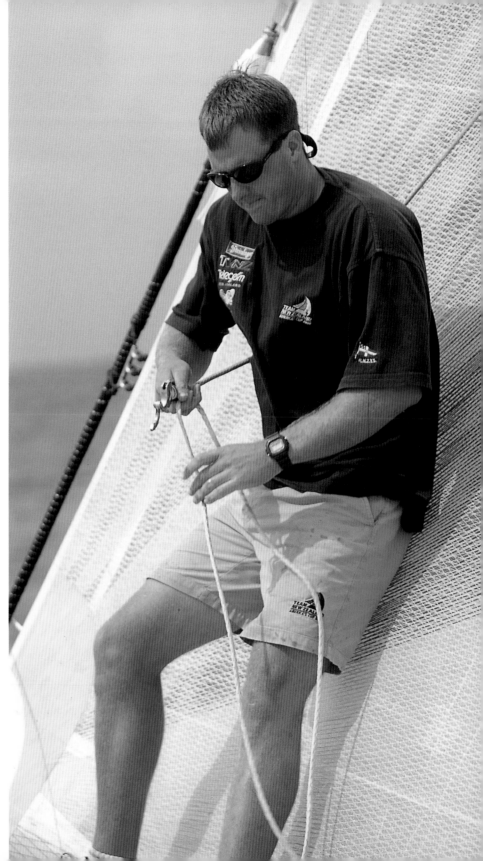

*New Zealander Laurie Davidson (right) was one of **Black Magic**'s principal hull designers. A veteran of Cups past, Davidson will play a key role in the 2000 event. Determined not to fall prey to complacency as the Australians did in their attempt to defend the 1987 Cup, TNZ has brought in fresh blood, such as crewman James Dagg (left) to keep their bid competitive. New advances in technology, strategy, and management are certain to push the 2000 Cup to a still higher level.*

the majority of Team Magic crew, has won the last three match-racing world championships in which he competed; 1992, 1993, and 1996. The fact that Butterworth, Coutts, Daubney, Fleury, and Phipps compete so regularly together should be an advantage for the larger Team New Zealand. Butterworth's involvement in the America's Cup since 1983 is a key advantage in balancing the rules issues and associated politics that can often be a disruptive factor for any team.

Twenty-six-year-old Dean Barker, and his primarily younger team, have also shown tremendous promise on the match-racing circuit, putting together a string of first and second finishes. He has joined test helmsman Murray Jones, who also enjoyed some high finishes in 1997 and 1998, as a viable backup for Coutts. Barker is working well with Olympic Laser representative Hamish Pepper, and this combination could well be being groomed for future America's Cup competition. It has been a focus of TNZ to invest in the future, with most of the new sailors being under the age of 26. James Dagg, Matthew Mitchell, and Cameron Appleton are three

such sailors who will have key roles to play in the future.

With the conditions in Auckland being more challenging, racing a 75-foot yacht with a crew of 16 people will demand a significantly higher level of fitness than was required in San Diego. The possibility of using a slightly different crew for stronger winds has not been missed, and it is notable that Dennis Conner used crew substitutions in Fremantle while the Kiwis stuck with the same crew for all races. It may be expected that TNZ will stack their race boat with bigger and stronger sailors for conditions of 20 knots or more.

Whether TNZ will be battle-hardened on the February day it meets the challenger on the America's Cup match starting line is a key question asked by both competitors and Cup followers. By match time, the challenger who wins the Louis Vuitton Cup and the right to sail against TNZ may by then have raced more than 70 races. Only time will tell if the Kiwis will be in the same fighting prime.

CHAPTER SEVEN

THE CHALLENGERS

The quest to win America's Cup 2000 began, in many respects, minutes after Team New Zealand's *Black Magic* crossed the finish line ahead of *Young America* on May 13, 1995. As the fifth and deciding race of the 29th Cup became history, and it was clear that the next contest would be played out on New Zealand waters, the first order of business was for the new defender to be challenged. Tradition, or at least a loose sense of history, dictates that the wheels of Cup organization do not begin to

New Zealand's victory in 1995 produced a wild celebration by the crew of Black Magic *and its many avid fans (left). Almost before the shouting had subsided the challenge process began, which will culminate in America's Cup 2000 in Auckland.*

turn until an official challenge is proffered and accepted.

Officially, any yacht club based anywhere in the world can challenge the defender, as long as the yacht club meets the criteria set out in the Deed of Gift. It is the defender's responsibility to select a "Challenger of Record," the designation given to the club that will then serve as a sort of clearinghouse for all the challengers and the procedural issues and questions that inevitably arise. The club also has the responsibility of running the challenger selection trials—no easy feat.

For their part, the defender—and there have been only three in almost 150 years of Cup racing—chooses a challenging club somewhat simpatico with its own overall vision. This has led to the establishment of what is known as the hip-pocket challenge, a predetermined arrangement between the club that appears to be the next defender and a club that has resolved to become an official challenger.

Sir Peter Blake, head of Team New Zealand, announced at the final press conference that his team had received and accepted the challenge from the New York Yacht Club, confirming a rumor that had spread through San Diego for days. The club was the Challenger of Record, and now what it needed was a syndicate.

Four options presented themselves. The three 1995 defense candidates (Koch's *America³*, Conner's *Stars & Stripes*, and John Marshall's *PACT '95*) had viable syndicates already formed. The New Yorkers could join forces with one of them or begin from scratch with their own organization. Negotiations began, and after lengthy talks the club decided to affiliate with Marshall and his group. Conner, now used to finding his own way when the New York Yacht Club looked elsewhere for a skipper, launched his challenge through the Cortez Racing Association in San Diego. Koch stepped to the sidelines recently vacated by the New Yorkers.

By the time the 1995 contenders had packed their gear, sold or stored their equipment, and left San Diego, talk of the 2000 event was beginning to drift through yacht clubs around the world. One of the first announcements was that there would be no defense trials, meaning that Team New Zealand would defend the trophy it had won. There were a number of reasons for this declaration, most of which had to do with the lim-

Team New Zealand's now famous **Black Magic** *dueled with Team Dennis Conner's* **Young America** *during the 1995 America's Cup match. The American defender proved to be no match for* **NZL-35,** *which performed flawlessly.*

ited resources of the small island nation. Although Chris Dickson and his Tag Heuer team had performed surprisingly well as a New Zealand challenger on a shoestring budget in 1995, the powers that be in Team New Zealand reasoned that a one-team, concentrated defense effort was the best utilization of the nation's sailing talent and budget.

With the defender announced, the focus in the sailing world turned to potential challengers. By January 31, 1998, 16 teams from 10 nations had deposited a quarter-million dollars each to officially declare themselves in the hunt—first for the Louis Vuitton Cup and then, if luck and skill held out, for the America's Cup. At the time of this writing, lack of funds forced the team from the U.S. Virgin Islands to merge with Team Dennis Conner, and the syndicates in Hong Kong and Britain canceled plans to travel to Auckland. Russia may or may not appear, and if it does, the team will attempt to race on a 1992-vintage boat.

Those teams that have made it through the fundraising eliminations appear to bring with them a number of strengths. Design and sailing skills and not a small measure of luck, as always, will determine the outcome of the racing.

It seems that every docksider's early pick in the Louis Vuitton sweepstakes is the team sponsored by Prada, the famous Italian fashion house. One of the first challengers to be formed, the team boasts the dream set-up—a single sponsor that takes care of the bills while all other aspects of the campaign can be carried out with singular concentration. That fact alone put the design, construction, and sailing operations in a class of their own and perhaps as much as 18 months ahead of all other challengers, with the possible exception of the New York Yacht Club's *Young America*.

The president and CEO of the Prada challenge is Patrizio Bertelli, husband of Miuccia Prada, whose grandfather founded the firm. A fierce competitor in both business and sailing (he owns the 1937 Olin Stephens-designed 12-meter *Nyala*), Bertelli has transferred that energy and spirit to the America's Cup, which in his view

Prada's first new boat for 1999-2000 was launched with appropriate fanfare in Punta Ala, Italy, on May 5 and is named **Luna Rossa.**

is much more than an advertising vehicle for Prada. "We are doing the America's Cup to win the America's Cup," he has said.

But money isn't Italy's only advantage. The design team is overflowing with talent, skill, and proven America's Cup experience. Argentinean German Frers' list of winning ocean-racing designs earned him a ticket to Milan to draw lines for the 1992 Il Moro di Venezia syndicate. The boat he and his team designed beat all challengers and took Italy into the America's Cup match for the first time in history. Although the trophy went to Bill Koch and his America[3] group, the *Il Moro* performance was strong enough to warrant a recall of Frers by Prada.

Joining Frers is American designer Doug Peterson. Peterson brings as impressive a Cup history to the design table as any marine architect working today. An integral part of the design team that drew 1992 winner *America[3]*, Peterson was then hired by Team New Zealand for the 1995 campaign. He shared the responsibility of creating the hull lines and the overall design concept of the black boats with Laurie Davidson.

*Miuccia Prada, the granddaughter of the company's founder, had the honor of christening the **Luna Rossa** (left). Patrizio Bertelli (right) is the leader of Italy's challenge and the CEO of the I.P.I. Spa group, the sole manufacturer and distributor of the Prada brand.*

Peterson is known for pushing the envelope, for exploring new concepts in design. Add to that his intimate knowledge of the winning boat designs from the past two America's Cups and it's easy to see why Prada was eager to hire him.

Team New Zealand also lost David Egan to Prada. Egan is known as a wizard on the computer and is responsible for computational codes and modeling. In Auckland he worked on appendages and concentrated on the hydrodynamics of the keel, its stem, and its wings, as well as the aerodynamics of the rig for Team New Zealand.

Filling out the Prada design team are German Frers Jr. and Guido Cavalazzi. Frers Jr. oversees the tank-test work outside of Rome, and Cavalazzi's major responsibility is the design of the sails.

The Prada team has a distinctly international flavor, but the syndicate came home for its helmsman, Francesco de Angelis, one of Europe's premier skippers. After his name was added to the roster, the first order of business for de Angelis was to gain match-racing experience. When selected by Prada, he was completely unfamiliar with this format as a helmsman.

His advancement to the semifinals of the U.S. Virgin Islands' contest illustrated his skill at the wheel and his

ability to learn quickly. But his uneven record since then speaks to the ever-increasing competition on the international match-racing circuit, known as the training ground for the America's Cup. Time and time again de Angelis and his match-racing team, which includes Torben Grael, a highly rated helmsman in his own right, raced against teams that will be competing in Auckland. How much experience was gained and how sharply the skills were tuned will become evident in the Hauraki Gulf.

While match racing may not be his forte, de Angelis' record in fleet racing is enviable. With roots in the Finn Class, he held a number of Italian, European, and World titles in the J24, Star, and One-Ton classes during the 1980s. In 1988 he took charge of the BRAVA team, a campaign that culminated in an Admiral's Cup championship in 1995, the first time an Italian team won. At the helm was de Angelis.

Few sailors racing today can duplicate Grael's record. Most recently he won the Olympic gold medal in the extremely competitive Star Class at the 1996 Games in Atlanta. He won a bronze medal in the same class at Seoul in 1988 and a silver medal in the Soling Class in 1984 at Los Angeles. He holds five One-Ton world cham-

Francesco de Angelis (left, discussing the progress of preparations with syndicate CEO Patrizio Bertelli) was selected as Prada's helmsman in 1996 and has devoted considerable time since then to the intricacies of match racing, the one-on-one format used in the America's Cup.

pion titles and has traveled the match-race circuit over the past two years with de Angelis as tactician.

Prada's sailing coach is Rod Davis, one of the most experienced match-racing and America's Cup sailors in the world. Originally from San Diego, he first appeared in Cup competition at age 21 as bowman aboard *Enterprise* in the 1977 defender trials. He coached the Australian challenge in 1980. In 1983 he sailed on *Defender*, again in the defense trials, and then was named helmsman of *Eagle* in the 1986/1987 Cup as a challenger. In 1992 he skippered *New Zealand* in all but two races, and three years later he was at the wheel of *oneAustralia*. His credentials also include Olympic gold (1984, Soling) and silver (1992, Star) medals, plus considerable professional match-racing experience and many victories.

Also bringing considerable depth of Cup experience to the Prada team is Laurent Esquier. As operations manager, he has similar responsibilities to those he had in 1992 for the Il Moro di Venezia syndicate. He knows New Zealand waters from his time as coach and operations manager with the first Kiwi challenge in 1986/1987, and he has on-board Cup experience, having crewed on the French teams in 1974 and 1977.

The Prada team and the two-boat campaign (sail numbers ITA45 and ITA48) they are conducting present a formidable challenge: money, experience, skills, desire. It's no wonder odds makers back the Italians, but how well all of that will translate into on-the-water performance against other teams is a story that will be told beginning in October 1999.

The force behind Japan's Cup efforts has been Tatsumitsu Yamasaki, an enthusiastic sailor and chairman of S&B foods, Asia's market leader in the spice importing business. When a challenge was first conceived some five years before the '92 event, Japan knew little about the game and had no Cup infrastructure on which to build—no boats, no sailors with Cup experience, no Cup-specific technology.

Understanding this, Yamasaki looked to New Zealand for support. The Kiwis had just completed a storied rookie effort by coming from nowhere to make it into the Louis Vuitton Cup finals before losing to Dennis Conner. To solve his no-boat problem, Yamasaki purchased the first two fiberglass 12-meters built by New Zealand. To help solve the lack of experience problem, he hired four Kiwis to form the core of Japan's first effort: Chris Dickson as skipper; John Cutler as tactician; Erle Williams, who had raced in Fremantle; and Mike Spanhake, a sailmaker and trimmer.

The Nippon Challenge made its America's Cup debut in 1992. It performed respectably, coming out of the Louis Vuitton Cup round robin as points leader before falling in the semifinals. The '92 effort was encouraging, and Yamasaki quickly joined the challengers for the 1995 contest. This time the approach was different. An emphasis on technology was behind a restructuring of the design and technical teams, with more Japanese recruited. Dickson left and formed the Tutukaka Challenge in New Zealand, while Cutler took his place behind the Nippon wheel. Match-racing star Makoto Namba came on board and was named skipper (but not helmsman) just before the challenger trials began, and Australian Peter Gilmour joined as coach and helmsman of the trial boat.

The team was the first to launch a new IACC boat, *JPN-30*, for the '95 event. The boat was tested against the '92 racer for almost a year before the final yacht was built. As in their first attempt to win the famed trophy, the Nip-

The Japanese challenges in 1992 and 1995 (right) both advanced to the semifinals, a showing this year's team is hoping to surpass.

Peter Gilmour (middle) has been sailing with an all-Japanese team on the international match circuit for several years as part of Team Brut and then under the auspices of sponsor Pizza-LA.

pon Challenge once again advanced to the Louis Vuitton Cup semifinals, but the quantum leap in boat speed hoped for in the new yacht was not there. The rebuilt *JPN-30* sailed to a 9–9 record before the newer *JPN-41* squeaked into the semis with a 2–4 record. The team lost all 11 races in the semifinals.

Although the '95 campaign was disappointing, Japan has made great strides in the sport. Where there had been no boats, no experience, no America's Cup infrastructure just a decade before, there is now a bona fide Cup community that counts as its assets five IACC yachts, 13 years of design knowledge, sailors who have been tested in intense

competition, and a strong core of sponsorship support.

So for the third consecutive America's Cup, Japan will challenge again. But soon after the announcement, Nippon was rocked by two events. Makoto Namba was lost at sea when a rogue wave washed him overboard during a race off Japan's coast. His loss was felt throughout the sailing world as he was widely considered one of the sport's true gentlemen. In his homeland the pain was especially sharp as he was known not only as a great sailor, but also as a great ambassador for his country. His outstanding leadership qualities will be sorely missed by the Nippon Challenge.

The other setback was jointly shared by financial markets throughout the world. When Japan's economy faltered, sparking the Asian economic crisis, Nippon Challenge's fund-raising efforts were severely crippled. Unlike the previous two campaigns, which were up and running at full speed as much as three years in advance of racing, Nippon 1999/2000 will forgo many preliminary training exercises in deference to a leaner budget. But the emphasis on technology, a mainstay of Nippon '92 and '95, remains intact.

The approach to design has been altered somewhat. Rather than a single individual heading the team, a committee was formed and given the responsibility of designing and building two new IACC boats. Whether funding allows both boats to actually be built is not clear at the time of this writing, but the design process has been under way since the spring of 1996. Coordinating the efforts of scientists, technicians, marine architects, students, and builders is Professor Hideaki Miyata of the Department of Naval Architecture and Ocean Engineering at the University of Tokyo.

The committee has relied heavily on computer modeling and CFD (computational fluid dynamics) tools to create some 50 designs that, after testing, evolved into five models that have been tank-tested. The Nippon team seems confident that its yacht development, combined with considerable research conducted on the wind and wave conditions on the Auckland racecourse, will produce an advanced racing yacht.

Who will steer and crew the yacht was resolved shortly after the '95 team returned to Japan from San Diego. Chairman Yamasaki recognized the qualities Peter Gilmour brought to the Nippon program both on and off the water by naming him skipper and helmsman for the new campaign. The decision was met with considerable approval by team veterans, who appreciate the Australian's skills and talents. For almost as long as Japan has been involved in the America's Cup, Gilmour has been ranked among the top five match-racing sailors in the world, often reaching number one. As sailing coach of Nippon and skipper of the trial horse in 1995, his contributions were significant.

While funding hasn't allowed Gilmour to mount a concentrated crew training effort as in the past, several years ago he formed a core team of Nippon Challenge sailors who have been regular competitors on the international match-racing circuit. Sponsored by Pizza-LA, the team has often raced its way into regatta finals and has emerged as champions in a number of tightly contested battles. In 1997 Gilmour and crew won the World Championship of Match Race Sailing and also achieved the number-one ranking, a position familiar to the skipper.

The fact that the Nippon Challenge has persevered through what has to be its darkest days is testament to the syndicate's strength. Perhaps more so than any other challenger, the team from Japan has already met, and passed, a number of severe tests. Having reached the semifinals of the Louis Vuitton Cup in its previous two attempts, Nippon presents a strong case as a potential finalist in Auckland.

Like Japan, Spain is a two-time veteran of the America's Cup, having raced in San Diego under the auspices of España 92 and Rioja de España 95. Unlike Japan, neither of the Spanish efforts gained a semifinal berth. Underfunded and late to build, both syndicates arrived on the racecourse with one-boat campaigns. In 1992, under the leadership of skipper Pedro Campos, team members had cause to believe they might have caught lightning in a bottle when they won their first two races. But reality soon set in when the stronger teams easily disposed of the rookie effort in round one, with margins ranging from 4 to more than 9 minutes at the finish.

Spain struggled through the challengers' second round, winning three races, but accumulating only 14 points to the leader's (New Zealand) 34. Perhaps most indicative of the difference between the haves and have-nots was the almost 14-minute beating the team suffered at the hands of *Il Moro di Venezia,* the eventual Louis Vuitton Cup winner. España 92 returned home after winning seven of its 21 races and finished fifth out of eight challengers. The performance was judged credible enough for them to try again in 1995.

Rioja de España never had a chance. The boat barely made it out of Spain in time to make it to the starting line in California. The team, once again led by Campos, had only two days of practice before the challenger trials began. They hardly knew their positions, much less how to get the full potential out of the boat. They were still testing sails and equipment during the races, tests their competitors completed months earlier. After losing its first 15 races, Spain's final numbers were 3–21. Those numbers don't really reflect the consistent improvement shown throughout the challenger trials, and the final race against *Nippon* was close throughout, proving just how far the Spaniards had come. At the finish line, just 13 seconds separated the two boats, and

Spain's 1995 yacht, **Rioja de España,** *was the last of the challengers to arrive in San Diego and was still testing sails and equipment during the early racing. The 0–15 start gave plenty of incentive to the 1999 team to arrange funding well in advance of the competition.*

Pedro Campos (right), who has been at the center of each of Spain's Cup challenges since the nation's first effort in 1992, selected Luis Doreste (left) to helm Spain's challenge in Auckland. Doreste is the owner of two Olympic gold medals in the 470 (1984) and Flying Dutchman (1992) classes.

Japan won the right to advance into the semifinals.

In hopes of results being different in Auckland, Spain has once again turned to Pedro Campos, but he is about the only constant this time around. Now the money appears to be in place, and the design team has been strengthened immeasurably. Two boats (sail numbers ESP-47 and ESP-56) will be built, and Campos will be joined in the cockpit with one of his country's most proven sailors. This time Spain wants to prove to the world it can compete on equal status with anyone.

More than $15 million have been raised, chiefly from government sources, the country's royal family, and repeat sponsor Telefonica. Like most America's Cup teams of today, a good part of the funds is being spent on design and technology. Where Japan's entry into the Cup wars began with the purchase of two New Zealand 12-meters, Spain's began with the purchase of designs by New Zealander Bruce Farr. Lead designer Joaquin Coello used those plans and the designs and test data from '92 to draw the lines for the '95 racer. But for the Auckland America's Cup, Coello has once again looked beyond his country's shores for design talent.

Spain has lacked resources in the design field, especially in big boats. With a keen understanding of this and with sufficient funds in place early enough to make strategic moves, Coello brought in one of the most renowned names in big-boat design. With many successes in a number of classes, Dutchman Rolf Vrolijk is a significant addition to the Spanish effort. A partner in the German firm of Judel/Vrolijk, the designer is reputed to have free reign to use his full creativity in planning the two racing yachts.

Unlike seven years ago, the design team now has a number of assets on which to rely. Although Vrolijk has never designed an America's Cup yacht, Coello has. There are also two Spanish-designed and -built IACC yachts. One will serve as a training platform for the 1999/2000 team after undergoing alterations to make her more in sync with the hull shape and appendages anticipated for New Zealand conditions.

The sailing team has also been bolstered by the addition of Luis Doreste, perhaps Spain's most accomplished sailor. The owner of two Olympic gold medals in the 470 (1984) and Flying Dutchman (1992) classes, Doreste has not had a great deal of match-racing experience in big boats, but his skills may be enough to compensate for this. There is the possibility he will emerge as the helmsman in Auckland, as Campos takes on more of a role in syndicate management and perhaps competes as a tactician.

While this edition of the sailing team might not be mistaken for grizzled veterans, neither should they be considered rookies. In 1992 that charge may have had validity, especially given their lack of time on board big boats or on the match-racing circuit. But the situation is different today. Campos and his racing team were frequent match-race competitors during the past few years, and the two Cup appearances have served the team well. Having reinforced so many areas of the challenge, it is almost unthinkable that Spain will suffer another 0-for-15 start in the New Zealand America's Cup.

FRANCE

When le défi Bouygues Telecom Transiciel syndicate sends its one-boat (sail number FRA46) campaign to the starting line in October, France will celebrate its 29th year of America's Cup competition. In 1970 Baron Marcel Bich, of the Bic pen and disposable lighter fortune, brought his country into the game in rather grand style. Fine wine and remarkable parties were more in evidence than sailing skills (France failed to win a race against Australia's *Gretel II* in the challenger trials), but Bich's white-glove entry laid a foundation for Cup challenges to come.

Bich's same boat lost in 1974 to Australia again, this time racing the new *Southern Cross*. In 1977, *France* was intended to be merely the trial horse for *France II*, but the new boat built of wood proved too slow, and the old war-horse was once again commissioned for battle. Mercifully, the yacht was retired after a three-Cup campaign that ended without a victory in 18 races. Bich experienced his first win in 1980 when *France 3* was well sailed by skipper Bruno Troublé into the finals against Australia. The Aussies advanced to the America's Cup match against Dennis Conner and *Freedom*, but

not before France took a race off them.

Bich then announced his retirement from the Cup and sold *France 3* to the film producer Yves Roussert-Rouard. Roussert-Rouard campaigned the yacht in the 1983 challenger trials, the first year they were sponsored by Louis Vuitton. Troublé, who has since gone on to head the Louis Vuitton activities associated with the Cup, was once again the helmsman. But his work as marketing director for Bic Marine prevented his full-time, on-board presence, and coupled with money problems and an inexperienced crew, the challenge was an also-ran.

The Baron Bich era gave way to the Marc Pajot era, which began with great promise but ended badly. A cel-

France is hoping to fare better with its current boat, 6th sens (right), than it did in 1995, when accusations of mismanagement, internecine battles, and severe damage to the yacht that was to be the trial horse more than offset the substantial budget and talented crew that Marc Pajot had been able to assemble.

ebrated helmsman in France, Pajot excelled in small and large boats, in round-the-buoy and round-the-world races, in monohulls and multihulls, in solo transatlantic competition and on yachts with large crews. After winning an Olympic silver medal in the Flying Dutchman Class, Pajot evolved into his country's highest paid athlete. He made his first Cup appearance in Fremantle in 1986. Backed by the first corporate single sponsor in Cup history, the instant photo concern KIS, he skippered a computer-conceived yacht sporting everyone's favorite name—*French Kiss*—and made it into the semifinals before falling to the Kiwis and their fiberglass speedster.

For the 1992 event in San Diego, Pajot found financial support from the Ville de Paris, whose mayor at the time, Jacques Chirac, is now France's president. The skipper repeated his Fremantle performance by racing his way into the semifinals, but once again he was eliminated during that round. Three years later Pajot arrived in San Diego with a huge budget, a crew of France's sailing elite, and his compatriots' expectations for Gallic success. But the effort was plagued by severe damage to the yacht that was to be the trial horse, the loss of that yacht's keel, internecine battles, accusations of mismanagement, and, in the end, an ineffectual racing record of 8–16. This time the team did not make it to the semifinals, and more than one French journalist called for Pajot's head.

For the Auckland America's Cup, it became clear early that Pajot was a man without a country, or at least without his own country. France would not back the skipper this time. As he looked toward Switzerland, his native land began a youth movement that produced a syndicate called Yaka, which initially promised a majority of crew members with ages of less than 25. In early training Luc Pillot, a rising star on the match-racing circuit, appeared to be on the fast track to be named helmsman. It was Pillot who, when asked what "Yaka" meant, responded that the word had no definite translation but was loosely interpreted to mean "just do it," an expression reminiscent of an American sneaker company's tag line.

No matter how the syndicate defined itself, from the beginning it appeared to have the strongest chance of getting Frenchmen to New Zealand. Two other syndicates were formed in the south of France, and they flirted with establishing ongoing campaigns, but fundraising problems forced a merger into what it now called the Le defi Sud.

Yaka was renamed after le défi Bouygues Telecom Transiciel signed on as the syndicate's sponsor. Bertrand Pacé, France's top-ranked match racer and 1994 world champion, replaced Pillot and will be at the wheel in Auckland. He has been involved in the past three America's Cups, most recently as tactician of the French boat in 1995. Money is tight. Syndicate head Luc Gelluseau is banking on advancement to the semifinals with a one-boat campaign, at which time he then foresees additional checks being written.

The design approach is similar to that of defender Team New Zealand. A team has been formed that includes designers and scientists. It is led by Philippe

Luc Gelluseau (left) has run the Corum sailing team since 1990 and is co-manager with Pierre Mas of le défi Bouygues Telecom Transiciel. France's highest ranked match racer, Bertrand Pacé (right), has been selected to command the racing team.

Paulu de la Barriere, whose Cup experience goes back to Baron Bich's *France 3*.

Meanwhile, although Marc Pajot leads his own campaign in Switzerland, he still has something to say about the French effort. Strapped for funds, Le defi Sud appears to have only one chance to make it to Auckland, and that chance, in the form of the IACC yacht the Swiss team has used for training, is controlled by Pajot. Originally planned for the 1995 Cup, the yacht was only partially finished when acquired by the Swiss. Le defi Sud's hope is to raise enough money to charter the yacht, but the syndicate must also deal with legal questions concerning how much of the yacht was rebuilt by Switzerland. It is possible that France will have two teams in Auckland, but the reality is that Le defi Sud would have little chance in a four-year-old boat against the new generation Cup yachts being built around the world. The better chance for a strong showing is le défi Bouygues Telecom Transiciel.

SWITZERLAND

As noted earlier, Marc Pajot has crossed the border into a landlocked country that perhaps few observers would have considered an America's Cup hopeful. But with its longstanding policy of neutrality, Switzerland presents an ideal profile for the French ex-patriot. And Pajot has made the most of this opportunity, forming an international team that features a German helmsman, an Italian tactician, a French designer, a Dutch-Australian technician, and crewmen from several European countries. All together, they form the Fast 2000 team.

Pajot's choice for helmsman drew immediate attention. Jochen Schumann, winner of three Olympic gold medals, is renowned in his country and respected by the international sailing community. He has excelled at every level of the sport. Pajot's decision to give the helm over to Schumann so he can concentrate on the syndicate leadership role has been generally viewed as a beneficial move. The employment as tactician of Enrico Chieffi, one of Italy's top sailors with Cup experience, also strengthens the team.

There is considerable optimism within the Swiss camp that the yacht will prove to be fast. Heading the design team is Philippe Briand, one of the most experienced Cup designers at work today. He has been teamed with Pajot since the days of *French Kiss*, the semifinalist in Fremantle. Briand is the author of five IACC racers, and the public relations spin on his new creation is that he has hit all the marks.

Much of the design work has been done by computer modeling, and Pajot and Briand are said to like what they see. Tank-testing has been done in England, at the same facilities that Team New Zealand uses; the Swiss believe them to be more accurate than facilities Briand has used in the past. Before the initial funds ran out, enough modeling and testing were done to allow the team to make a final decision on which design to build. They are confident they have a competitive boat. There are even whispers of a breakthrough.

The yacht Marc Pajot and his crew have been training on was originally designed for the 1995 America's Cup and may be chartered by the Esprit-Sud team from France.

The team did spend some time on New Zealand waters, but most of their training has been on Swiss lakes. The new boat is designed and built specifically for the Hauraki Gulf. With funding in place to complete the construction, the question that remains is whether the sailors have enough time on board to tune it, and themselves, properly. It is a question well asked of many of the challengers.

Philippe Briand (opposite), head of FAST 2000's design team, is one of the most experienced Cup designers at work today. Jochen Schumann (above, left), designated helmsman for the syndicate, has won three Olympic gold medals and is renowned as one of the best sailors in the world. Marc Pajot (above, right) made his America's Cup debut in 1986 for France and will be in New Zealand as head of the Swiss syndicate.

AUSTRALIA

An America's Cup event in the Southern Hemisphere without an entry from Australia is unthinkable. Since 1962, when *Gretel* took a race off *Weatherly*, the Aussies have been major players in the Cup game and have written their own extraordinary history. Designer Alan Payne, chief architect of *Gretel* and *Gretel II*, demonstrated an innovative brilliance in his work which gave his country Cup creditability worldwide.

Although the country suffered through winless contests with *Dame Pattie* (1967), *Southern Cross* (1974) and *Australia* (1977), a strong foundation was being built. *Gretel's* race win in the America's Cup match was followed by one in 1970 (*Gretel II*) and another in 1980 (*Australia*). While this may not seem too impressive, consider that as a challenger, the Australian yachts beat back all their competition to advance to the Cup match. The final hurdle

Stars & Stripes *(right) of the United States met Australia's* Kookaburra III *(left) in the 1987 Cup off the western coast of Australia. The U.S. boat prevailed, sending the event to California.*

remained the Americans, with their unequaled depth of experience, talent, and resources.

That hurdle was overcome in 1983 by syndicate head Alan Bond's money, designer Ben Lexcen's wing keel, the syndicate's executive director Warren Jones' political savvy, and skipper John Bertrand's sailing and leadership talent. The great victory that brought the end to America's 132-year winning streak pumped new life into the Cup and made the event a truly international competition. When the tiny town of Fremantle in Western Australia opened for America's Cup business in 1986, some 13 challengers, the largest number ever, were waiting on the threshold. The racing that took place in the wild and woolly Indian Ocean was an unqualified success, viewed by many as the best America's Cup in history. Australia played the perfect host, extending its gracious hospitality to all visitors by not only offering what may have been the perfect venue but by playing the friendly villain in Dennis Conner's emotional comeback scenario. For America's Cup afficionados, it was the best of times.

Some observers speculate that had Australia not won

the trophy in 1983, many of the challengers who have since entered the game might not have done so without the proof that America could be beaten. After all, the United States kept the Cup for 132 years, and before 1983 the matches had never really been even close. Since that time, Japan, Spain, Switzerland, and New Zealand have mounted actual campaigns, while Russia, Hong Kong, Germany, and the U.S. Virgin Islands have formed syndicates later disbanded because of lack of funds. Australia can be thanked for keeping the game alive.

Add to the country's history the most extraordinary event in America's Cup history. The dramatic sinking of *oneAustralia* while racing in 1995 off the coast of California generated not only worldwide front-page head-

lines but also the realization of a need for balance between design and engineering innovation and just plain safety. While the light winds and relatively gentle wave conditions in San Diego allowed designers and builders some latitude in which to push the envelope, New Zealand presents a completely different set of challenges. No doubt the *oneAustralia* experience played a part in the thinking of every designer, technician, engineer, and builder who is sending a boat to Auckland.

Australia is poised to make history once again in the person of Syd Fischer, the fifth attempt by the man called "Nails," a record equal to that of Sir Thomas Lipton. His Young Australia 2000 campaign also features the youngest skipper ever to helm an America's Cup entry—Sydney native James Spithill, age 19. True to the syndicate's name, and comparable to the approach of France's le défi Bouygues Telecom Transiciel, the crew will consist of 11 sailors aged 18 to 22 and four experienced mentor sailors. The young sailors are being selected from various youth programs at Australia's leading yacht clubs.

Fischer's attempts in 1983 (*Advance*) and 1992 (*Challenge Australia*) are perhaps better forgotten as they

were well off the pace. But his 1987 (*Sydney Steak 'n' Kidney*) and 1995 (*Sydney*) had the makings of real contenders. In fact, there are those within the Cup community who still believe that *Steak 'n' Kidney* had the potential to be the fastest boat in Fremantle had it been allowed to develop fully under the Royal Perth Yacht Club's defense selection series. Fischer still holds the Club responsible for Australia's inability to defend the Cup against Conner.

This time he is the only challenger from his country, and he is beholden to no one. Fischer is well known in sailing circles as his own man, an individual who not only marches to his own drummer but pays no heed to the beat. As an official challenger who paid the quarter-million-dollar bill to join the party, he has the right to make his opinions known on Cup issues. And he has. More than once.

When the prices for syndicate compound space in Auckland were originally announced, he led the protest over what was seen as exorbitant rates. Although they have been reduced and the real estate has been leased, Fischer has said his challenge will operate from their own barge moored in the harbor just off the pricey Cup Village. (It has also been reported that he later made inquiries about compound space alongside his fellow competitors.)

Fischer also led the dissent over some unnamed syndicates' second thoughts about the semifinal format after challengers had voted to allow six boats into the competition. And he insisted upon clarification of money distribu-

The sinking of oneAustralia (right) off the coast of California in 1995 generated international headlines and prompted renewed focus on the need to balance safety with design innovation, a lesson surely not lost on the competitors in Auckland.

tion from television and other licensing rights. It is fair to say that he has not gone quietly into his fifth campaign, but then again, who more than Syd Fischer has earned the right to question the rules?

This is not a man who is accustomed to either losing or being told what to do. In sport he has competed in and won almost all of the most prestigious ocean races, including the Admiral's Cup, the One-Ton Cup, the Kenwood Cup, the Fastnet Race, and, perhaps most important to him, the Sydney-Hobart Race. He also excelled on the rugby field. In business he is known as a tough negotiator (hence the name Nails), and few, if any, have had the better of him.

Also involved in Young Australia 2000 is Sir James Hardy, whose Cup experience goes all the way back to when he drove *Gretel II* in the 1970 match. Hardy is revered in the Australian sailing community, and his soft-spoken manner seems the perfect foil to Fischer's more excitable demeanor.

No doubt by the time the team crosses the Tasman to compete in Auckland, the focus will be on Spithill, on the young sailors, on the racing yacht, and on the team's chances for advancement. But there is no question that the spotlight will still shine on Syd.

UNITED STATES

ALOHA RACING

"Abracadabra" is defined by Webster's Dictionary as a "magical word once held to avert disease or disaster." Dr. Jim Andrews, chairman of the Aloha Racing Challenge for the America's Cup, has used the word to name his string of ocean-racing yachts over the past decade, and so far disaster has been averted. The good doctor must have uttered the word more than once in an effort to restore his ailing syndicate to health rather than see it succumb to the disease of insufficient funds.

Andrews' affiliation with the four-billion-dollar healthcare concern called HealthSouth, with more than 1,900 medical and rehabilitation centers worldwide, helped restore financial stability when the company agreed to sponsorship. The infusion of dollars was enough to complete the design and construction programs that will produce two IACC racers (sail numbers USA50 and USA54) and get the team from Hawaii to New Zealand. It is, indeed, a magical time for Andrews' and Hawaii's first-ever Cup campaign.

If Andrews is a novice at the game, his chosen skipper John Kolius is a veteran. Often acting as helmsman on the *Abracadabra,* Kolius has worked well with Andrews since 1990. His skills at the wheel of a sailboat first received international recognition in 1983 when he was brought into the Defender/Courageous group. They were attempting to win selection by the New York Yacht Club to defend the trophy against a fleet of seven challengers. The original plan by Defender principals Tom Blackaller and Gary Jobson was to use the 10-year-old *Courageous* as a sparring partner to prepare their yacht and crew for Dennis Conner and his Freedom '83 campaign. But Kolius changed those plans when he found the speed in the aging doyenne of U.S. Cup 12-meters that the brand new *Defender* lacked.

Kolius and *Courageous* advanced to the finals of the defense trials where they met Conner and *Liberty.* The new kid on the block with the old boat continued to per-

*The crew of **Abracadabra 2000** posed in front of a mural painted by the renowned marine artist Wyland. His work is also prominently displayed on the hull of the racing boats.*

form well, but Conner and his new boat performed better and received the tip of the straw hat from the club's selection committee. Although Kolius was sent home, the way he had handled both his boat and himself impressed the New Yorkers. After Conner and *Liberty* lost to *Australia II* and its wing keel in the biggest upset in America's Cup history, the club suddenly found itself in the unfamiliar position of challenger. Eager to reclaim the trophy that had become synonymous with their organization, the club turned to Kolius to lead the way to Fremantle.

Unwittingly, Kolius found himself in the center of a controversy that reflected the club's inability to adjust to the role of challenger. The club signed contracts with sailmakers North and Sobstad, apparently forgetting that their chosen skipper was a partner in his own sailmaking concern, Ulmer/Kolius. When Kolius was asked to sign an agreement that stated he wouldn't build sails for his own campaign, he understandably refused. This disagreement, added to internal political strife and syndicate management problems, brought to the surface a number of conflicts, and Kolius saw no alternative other than to resign.

As a result of some old-fashioned back-room politicking by some Texas money men who had been in the Kolius corner from the beginning, the club agreed to a reorganization. Kolius returned, but what had once been the stronghold of Cup defense had displayed its weakness as a challenger, and the campaign arrived in Australia somewhat stunned and wounded. Its failure to advance to even the semifinals (losing out to *French Kiss* by one point) proved unbearable for many of the club's members and was a contributing factor to the more than 10-year hiatus from Cup competition.

While the New York Yacht Club stepped to the sidelines, Kolius stayed involved in Cup campaigns as coach of the Il Moro di Venezia team in 1992 and the America[3] women's team in 1995. But undoubtedly the desire to fulfill the promise he exhibited in 1983 pushed him to return as skipper and helmsman. Yet the lessons he learned from the Fremantle experience surely taught him that any involvement in an on-board leadership position had to be done under his own terms. That opportunity presented itself in Hawaii with Dr. Andrews.

Under the official auspices of the Waikiki Yacht Club, with the majority of funding from HealthSouth, Aloha Racing was established to "bring the America's Cup to Paradise." It seems an ideal set-up for Kolius, some 3,000 miles from the U.S. mainland, away from the glare of media and second-guessers. He has complete control of the sailing operations and receives no interference from Waikiki. But perhaps most important, the team believes the wind and wave conditions are very similar to those in Auckland. Unlike many of the other challengers, Aloha Racing did not train in New Zealand prior to the Louis Vuitton Cup, but this may not be a disadvantage if their home base proves out their theory.

Designers Andy Dovell and Ian Burns, veterans of the design teams that produced *oneAustralia* in 1995 and

Spirit of Australia in 1992, have gone the computer-modeling and tank-testing routes in the absence of a syndicate-owned IACC boat. The team's first boat was launched in early June as the second yacht was completing construction. Name? *Abracadabra 2000,* of course. Further proof Kolius aims to avert the disaster that befell him the last time he ventured Down Under.

Dr. Jim Andrews is one of America's leading orthopedic surgeons and an avid sailor. His contributions to the Hawaiian syndicate have been immeasurable.

AmericaOne

Things looked pretty good in early 1996, when the venerable St. Francis Yacht Club, hard on the shores of San Francisco Bay, announced that it was giving official sanction to an America's Cup syndicate named AmericaOne, led by favorite son Paul Cayard. Cayard, a veteran of three America's Cup campaigns and a perennial star on the match-racing circuit, introduced James H. Clark as AmericaOne's chairman, a position he also held at Netscape Communications, the Internet browser company he had co-founded. In succeeding weeks additional personnel were announced that fit that mold.

Joining the group was designer Bruce Nelson, who traced his Cup origins to the Dennis Conner design team who produced the victorious boat coming out of Fremantle. He also worked with Conner on his 1988 catamaran defense and helped design the *Young America* yacht Cayard had steered in the '95 Cup. Laurent Esquier came on board as operations director. He worked with Conner in '83, is credited with teaching the crew of the first New Zealand Challenge how to handle 12-meter yachts in 1986/1987, and was with *Il Moro* in 1992.

As the team began to form, it presented a strong profile. Fund-raising prospects appeared solid, drawing on the wealthy yacht club membership, the San Francisco corporate community, and nearby Silicon Valley.

But within six months, things turned south. Clark resigned to devote more time to Netscape. Esquier left when Italy's Prada made him an offer he couldn't refuse. Several marketing managers came and went. Another Cup syndicate, America True, set up shop just across the Bay, undercutting AmericaOne's solo position in the San Francisco area. Money dried up, and rumors of the effort's ending spread along international docks.

After several tense weeks of meetings and strategy sessions, the ship was righted. St. Francis member George "Fritz" Jewett Jr. took over as vice chairman of the board of directors, and some semblance of order was restored. Jewett brought some 25 years of America's Cup experi-

AmericaOne's lead boat (right) will face stiff competition from the other U.S. syndicates as well as from a talented group of overseas challengers.

ence to the position. In 1974 he served as co-chairman of the Intrepid syndicate, then chairman of Enterprise in 1977. From 1980 to 1995 he supported Dennis Conner in a number of capacities, and Conner credits him with getting him back into Cup competition after 1983's loss to Australia when the skipper contemplated quitting the Cup for good. Jewett is one of the most savvy Cup individuals in the world.

Yet just as some of the holes in the leaking syndicate were being plugged, Cayard announced he would skipper *EF Language* in the Whitbread Round-the-World Race. It was a tremendously risky move to leave a fledgling Cup campaign at a vulnerable time. But the gamble paid off when Cayard became the first American to win the grueling contest, collecting valuable media coverage for more than a year. During stopovers, Cayard flew home to bolster fund-raising activities.

In less than 90 days from the conclusion of the Whitbread, AmericaOne closed on two significant sponsorships, Telcordia Technologies/SAIC and Ford Motor Company. Add to those the Hewlett-Packard Company, and it's clear that AmericaOne will be a force to be reckoned with in New Zealand.

Yet true to the seesaw nature of the campaign, bad news has been mixed with the good. Steve Erickson, one of Cayard's closest friends and longtime crew member, was coaxed away by Prada to help coach. Kimo Worthington, a Bay area resident and member of the America[3] team in both '92 and '95, defected to archrival Young America. Cayard was stung by the two exits, but when rumors began to swirl that John Kostecki was being wooed by Young America, he fought hard to keep the tactician in the AmericaOne fold.

Kostecki won the Olympic silver medal in the Soling Class in 1988 and has been among sailing's elite ever since. In 1997 he won the Mumm 36 World Championship, the One-Design 48 Championship, and the Malaysia Challenge Grand Prix. He also sailed in the Whitbread aboard *Chessie Racing* as co-helmsman/tactician and is credited with improving the boat's performance significantly.

Kostecki is joined on the AmericaOne sailing team by a number of other world-class sailors including Terry Hutchinson, Josh Belsky, Curtis Blewett, and Sean Clarkson.

Nelson has remained on board as the principal designer. His experience is a key component to AmericaOne's hopes. Before joining Conner's design team for the Fremantle Cup, he won recognition for several successful ocean-racing yachts. His work on *Stars & Stripes* was his first ever on a 12-meter and likewise on the 60-foot catamaran in 1988. In 1992 he was involved in the Partnership for America's Cup Technology (PACT), which was established as a reservoir of scientific and technological knowledge and resources from which the

In February 1999, the AmericaOne team sparred with fellow San Francisco syndicate America True in the waters off New Zealand (right). Paul Cayard (far left) hopes to reach the Cup match for the third consecutive time and add the trophy to his recent Whitbread victory. Bruce Nelson (left) heads up the AmericaOne design team.

defense syndicates could draw. PACT developed into PACT '95, and Nelson served as the lead designer on *Young America,* the boat Team Dennis Conner used in the America's Cup match against Team New Zealand. Cayard was the helmsman.

As the architect of the boat that lost to New Zealand 5–0, Nelson knows better than most what the challengers are up against. The Kiwis have a huge head start on everyone attempting to win the trophy, but Nelson may have the best idea of exactly what that head start entails.

No doubt considerable time has been spent comparing his design to that of the black boats.

Considering that Cayard has been behind the wheel in both the '92 and '95 America's Cup matches, the only two contests that have used IACC yachts, it is fair to say he comes to Auckland with the most experience of all the challengers. How much of an edge that will give him and his team will be answered on the Hauraki Gulf, but at this writing many odds makers see *AmericaOne* in the Louis Vuitton Cup semifinals.

UNITED STATES

AMERICA TRUE

Dawn Riley is arguably the best-known woman sailor in America. Adding to her portfolio of two Whitbread Round-the-World Races and positions on two America's Cup teams, she is using her high-profile experience to become the first woman to manage a Cup team. As CEO and captain of *America True,* affiliated with the San Francisco Yacht Club, Riley has put together a co-ed team that is a mixture of sailors with and without Cup experience. Her credo has been to select the best person for the job, regardless of gender.

While the focus of America True has certainly been on preparing for the races in Auckland, the syndicate has also designed a program that uses sailing to teach at-risk youth the fundamentals of team-building and operating a sailboat. It is a noble goal that has been applauded by local politicians and editorialists, and one

America True's training yacht carries on its hull a rendering of the Golden Gate Bridge, one of the most distinctive landmarks in the syndicate's home city of San Francisco.

that well illustrates the full potential of the sport.

In the early days of America True, it was questionable just how successful Riley and her philosophies would be. Altruism is one thing, but finding the millions of dollars needed to fund a campaign is another. Lucky for Riley that G. Christopher Coffin shared her vision. In early 1997 he came on board as a significant contributor and assumed the position of chief operating officer. According to America True, "The combination of Mr. Coffin's entrepreneurial experience, interest in technology, and passion for sailing have made bringing back the Cup an all-consuming project for Mr. Coffin and his family."

Coffin has an extensive background in communications technology and has reaped the rewards of selling a company he founded in the mid-'80s to U.S. Robotics. He now heads a venture capital group that funds technology companies. According to syndicate members and outside observers, his business and financial savvy is the major reason for America True's success in the fundraising arena and its assurance of a place on the starting line in Auckland.

The combination of Riley and Coffin has attracted both dollars and talent to the team. Making good on her promise of a co-ed team, Riley has recruited experienced Cup campaigners from the 1995 America³ women's team. Leslie Egnot has signed on as tactician. Behind the wheel in the last Cup, she brings a wealth of sailing experience as well as a knowledge of New Zealand waters, having lived there since 1972. She is joined by fellow Cubers Merritt Carey on the foredeck and trimmer Katie Petti-bone. Liz Baylis, an experienced big-boat sailor, will perform cockpit duties.

New Zealander John Cutler will steer. A 1988 Olympic bronze medalist in the demanding Finn Class, he was tactician and then helmsman for the Nippon Challenge in 1992 and 1995 respectively. He is a veteran of the international match-racing circuit, competing at a top level during the past decade.

Ben Beer, a resident of St. Thomas in the U.S. Virgin Islands, also is frequent crew on match races and will begin racing with America True after he competes in the Pan American Games in Finns. He'll work the foredeck at the America's Cup.

What may prove to be America True's greatest asset is more than five years of technical research reportedly

America True's Dawn Riley (right) worked the line (left foreground), with helmsman John Cutler at the wheel and tactician Leslie Egnot next to him in blue fleece. She is the first female CEO of an America's Cup team in the event's long history.

Leslie Egnot (far left) made her America's Cup debut in 1995 on the America³ women's team. She will serve in America True's afterguard. Buddy Melges (left) is the only American to have won an Olympic gold medal and an America's Cup title. He is America True's sailing coach. The team spent several months training on the Cup course in New Zealand. Crew member Katie Petibone (opposite) trimmed a sail off Rangatoto Island.

worth $60 million and developed by Bill Koch's America³ syndicate. The research helped create two fast-racing yachts, 1992 Cup winner *America³* and *Mighty Mary* in 1995. One of the design team members who worked on that project was Phil Kaiko, who also worked in the oneAustralia program in '95. Kaiko is the chief designer for *America True*.

And another asset from *America³* is Buddy Melges, America's dean of sailors. Only he and Kiwi Russell Coutts can claim ownership of an Olympic gold medal (Buddy's in Soling Class) and an America's Cup victory. A

few of his other sailing accomplishments include two Star World championships; a Pan Am Games gold medal in the Flying Dutchman Class; and five E-Scow and seven Skeeter ice-boat national championships. He has been selected as the Rolex Yachtsman of the Year three times.

Riley has proven a winner in the past and demonstrated her leadership abilities for more than a decade. Her selection of talent for the Cup is commendable, if yet unproven as a team. Like all challengers, the success of *America True* will probably be determined by just how fast a boat is designed and built (sail number USA51).

No one will be seen on the America's Cup course beginning in October 1999 with more experience in the game than Dennis Conner. It is arguable that no other individual has had a greater impact on the America's Cup than "DC." When he takes his team to the starting line in Auckland for the 1999/2000 competition, he will be sailing in his eighth America's Cup. He is the only man ever to have won the trophy four times and lost it twice.

Conner is often said to have single-handedly changed Cup preparations from a summer avocation to a full-time occupation. It is a charge he denies, but there is no question that he was instrumental in establishing the long campaign in which crew and sail training stretched from a few months to a period of more than a year. Conner was also in the forefront of the move from amateur status to commercial sponsorship. Other skippers and syndicate

Dennis Conner was all smiles as Paul Cayard lifted the Louis Vuitton Cup in 1995, signifying victory in the challenger selection trials and advancement to the America's Cup match.

heads may have come to the party with a great deal more money, but few have been better at garnering financial support in corporate board rooms and in the living rooms of the wealthy than Dennis Conner.

Like many individuals who have achieved the pinnacle of their chosen endeavor, Conner has been involved in more than a few controversies and has collected his detractors through the years. But it is rare to ever hear anything but praise and almost reverence from anyone who has ever campaigned with him. "My guys," as Conner calls his crew, often refer to their skipper's motivational skills when explaining their deep loyalty to him.

There are innumerable stories of Conner as a boy walking the docks of the San Diego Yacht Club, asking anyone with a mast on his boat if he needed crew. He had decided at a young age to learn everything he could about the sport, and he dedicated himself to that education. He became so familiar to the members of the club that he was offered a junior membership—the youngest person ever to join. Conner's name first drew attention from the sailing world as a Star sailor. This almost 23-foot boat

Bill Trenkle (left) has raced with Conner for years and heads to Auckland as operations manager for the American challenger.

epitomizes real sailing to Conner. To this day, he believes his five victories in the 1977 Star Worlds (he also won in 1971) are his greatest accomplishment in the sport. He also believes that Star sailors are a hitch above all others on sailing's food chain.

Over the years Conner has collected a room full of trophies, including an Olympic bronze medal in the Tempest Class, but it is his America's Cup racing that has made him a legend. First invited by Ted Turner to join him in the cockpit of *Mariner* for the defender trials of 1974, Conner quickly exhibited his skills and was promoted to starting helmsman aboard *Courageous*, the eventual Cup victor. In 1980 he skippered *Freedom* to victory, lost aboard *Liberty* in '83, won in Fremantle three years later, countered Michael Fay's big boat with a catamaran in '88, lost in the defender trials to Bill Koch's *America*[3] in '92, and lost the Cup match in '95 to the Kiwis.

For more than a quarter-century, Conner has been at the forefront of sailing's most prestigious regatta, and one would think everything there is to be known about the man is on public display. But just the opposite is true. A 1987 *Time* magazine profile of Conner perhaps put it best: "No more enigmatic character presides over any sport. At the top of his game, Conner can eat with Nicklaus, drink with Namath, offend with McEnroe, spend with Marcos, and lose with Napoleon."

And for the New Zealand event, Team Dennis Conner is perhaps the greatest enigma of all the challengers. Almost all that was known about this group until just a few months before the Louis Vuitton Cup was that Conner was among the official challengers. While most of his would-be opponents were flooding media fax machines and e-mail addresses with details of their progress in fund-raising, design, team building, and crew training, Conner sat silent. As usual, rumors stalked him: he has no money; he is fully funded; he has no designers; he has a secret design team; he isn't going to Auckland; he's moved to Auckland permanently.

In the spring of '99, Conner's longtime lieutenant Bill Trenkle finally set the record straight—sort of. It was announced that Peter Holmberg, America's top-ranked match racer and former head of the dying U.S. Virgin Islands Challenge, was joining Conner. Then came word that Ken Read, one of America's bright young sailors with '95 Cup experience, was selected as helmsman. He and Holmberg then hit the match-race circuit together, and with the Virgin Islander at the wheel they won the Congressional Cup.

Although the full team has not been announced at this writing, Conner has many of "his guys" waiting by the phone. Contrary to his lengthy training programs of the past, Conner's philosophy now appears to be something along the line of, "We all know how to race a sailboat, just give me a good boat." He's relying on the design talent of John Reichel to do just that. Reichel was part of the design teams of both *America*[3] and *oneAustralia*, and in

Peter Holmberg (right) was the co-founder of the U.S. Virgin Islands America's Cup challenge before merging with Team Dennis Conner. He will be in the afterguard during racing in Auckland. Dennis Conner (left) has been called Mr. America's Cup and for good reason. He will be making his eighth appearance in the event when he and his team travel to New Zealand.

partnership with Jim Pugh has designed a number of trophy winners.

While some of the questions surrounding Conner's eighth run for the Cup have been answered, many remain. Will the man who invented the two-boat campaign be handicapped by building just one boat (sail number USA55, the same number that adorned his *Stars & Stripes* in his Fremantle comeback victory)?

Conner will be 56 years old during the challenger trials and some wonder if his more relaxed approach to Cup preparations may be a concession to age. Detractors point to the calendar to explain his 19th place in the 1998 Etchells Worlds, a regatta he has formerly done well in. Supporters point out when he was at the helm of Toshiba in the Whitbread, he finished the leg in second place. They will also remind a listener that Buddy Melges steered *America*³ to victory in 1992 at the age of 62. But one wonders if Conner's decision to hire two hot-shot helmsmen in Holmberg and Read is a signal he won't be behind the wheel in Auckland.

Somehow that seems an impossibility, as hard to believe as any modern America's Cup without a Team Dennis Conner.

On paper, the New York Yacht Club's Young America entry looks like the overwhelming favorite of all the challengers, Italy's Prada included. Begin with the club, history-rich in the game and hungry after its decade on the sidelines during Cup competition. While major corporate sponsorship has not materialized at this writing, the club's wealthy membership has paid the bills through individual giving.

At the head of the effort is John Marshall, who dates his Cup involvement back to 1974 with *Intrepid*. In 1977 he steered *Enterprise* on downwind legs in the defense trials, and in 1980 he teamed with Dennis Conner in a Cup partnership that lasted until 1992 and garnered three victories. In '92 he headed the Partnership for America's Cup Technology (PACT), and in '95 he led what was alternately called PACT '95 and Young America. He serves as president and chief executive officer of the Young America Challenge.

Marshall graduated from Harvard with a degree in biochemistry and has also studied at the Rockefeller Institute and Stevens Institute of Technology. His scientific background served him well as manager of the *Stars & Stripes* design teams in the 1987 and 1988 Cup events. His sailing background includes winning an Olympic bronze medal in 1972 in the Dragon Class and as mainsail trimmer aboard *Freedom* ('80) and *Liberty* ('83). These dual disciplines give him a solid foundation as the man most responsible for organizing Young America.

On the design side Marshall hired two of the most experienced and recognized names in the sailing world. Perhaps better known as the undefeated skipper of *Patient Lady* in four consecutive Little America's Cups (international catamaran regattas) from 1977 to 1982, winning the trophy back from Australia in 1996, Duncan MacLane is the syndicate's design/technology manager. According to Young America, "MacLane manages the primary design areas of hull form, appendages, spars, sails, deck layout, mechanical systems, and composite structural engineering as well as support technologies such as free surface computational fluid

*Known as **The Mermaid** when the yacht sailed in the 1995 America's Cup, the Bruce Nelson-designed racer served as one of Young America's training yachts in the lead up to 1999/2000.*

dynamics for hull development and tank and wind tunnel testing for appendages." MacLane's experience in the Cup arena includes being co-designer of *Heart of America* in 1987 and design team leader of the *Stars & Stripes* catamaran in 1988.

The syndicate refers to Farr Yacht Design, Ltd. as its principal designer. The president and founder of the concern, Bruce Farr, may be the most sought-after racing sailboat designer in the world. His firm's dominance of major championships for almost 20 years is a story often told by happy owners around the globe. Farr was on the design teams that created New Zealand's first America's Cup entry in 1987, Michael Fay's big boat in 1988, New Zealand's Challenge in 1992, and Chris Dickson's *Tag Heuer* in 1995. Failure to win the Cup is the one outstanding blemish on an otherwise stellar career, and there is little doubt his work for Young America is receiving his most intense attention.

Skipper Ed Baird leads the sailing team. He received international recognition in 1995 as sailing coach of Cup winner Team New Zealand, as skipper of the victorious team that won the World Championship of Match Racing, as the number-one ranked match-racer, and as the recipient of the Rolex Yachtsman of the Year award. For Young America, Baird oversees crew recruitment and has helped organize an on-water team that boasts 17 Cup victories among its members. They include Stu Argo; Tom Burnham; Steve Calder; Bill Cambell; Jamie Gale and Ross Halcrow, both members of Team New Zealand in 1995; Hartwell Jordan; Tony Rey; Grant Spanhake; and Kimo Worthington. Baird has also been an integral part of the research and

Floridian Ed Baird is the designated helmsman for the New York Yacht Club's Young America challenge.

development phase of the syndicate's agenda by managing the sailing side of the two-boat testing program.

Young America has used two of the better 1995 International America's Cup Class yachts as their training platforms. *Young America*, the race boat used by the PACT '95 group and later sailed by Team Dennis Conner in the Cup match, was part of the assets turned over to the new syndicate. The acquisition of the Farr-designed *Tag Heuer* provided the second boat on which sail, gear, and crew training has taken place on the waters off Rhode Island in 1997 and 1998. Two-boat testing has been de rigueur in Cup preparations since 1980, when *Freedom* and *Enterprise* jousted with each other, testing more than a hundred sails, all manner of equipment, and crew members during almost six months of training before the defender trials even began. Since then, every America's Cup victor (save the '88 catamaran) has been the product of at least a two-boat campaign, and most competitors have run similar programs. When New Zealand introduced the concept of building two boats from the same fiberglass mold for the Fremantle Cup, the game changed once again.

Complementing Young America's on-the-water testing is the syndicate's reliance on computer modeling, tank testing and wind tunnel work, all encouraged by Marshall the scientist. Like almost all Cup contenders operating today, the syndicate also uses velocity prediction programs (VPPs), one of the most important design tools. VPPs give designers

Bruce Farr (far left) is considered one of the world's foremost racing yacht designers. His America's Cup boats have been involved in every event since New Zealand's famous fiberglass 12-meters in 1986. His talents are in the employ of Young America for America's Cup 2000. Jim Brady (near left) was Team Dennis Conner's navigator in the 1995 Cup and will sail with Young America in New Zealand.

the ability to estimate the maximum potential speed of a sailboat in a given wind condition, which in turn allows them to compare two or more designs.

Dr. Jerry Milgram, a professor at the Massachusetts Institute of Technology and one of Bill Koch's designers in 1992 and 1995, is a true believer in VPPs. He has brought that belief to Young America for this America's Cup, as well as the use of the sailing dynamometer, a model that measures sail forces directly on a sailboat. On-board computers record outputs from sailing instruments that provide wind speed and direction, boat speed, heel angle, and heading, among other measurements. When this data is compared against that from other designs, the result is the most accurate VPPs modern technology can achieve. How well Milgram, Marshall, MacLane, Farr, and the rest of the design team interpret that data and translate it to the builders at Goetz Custom Boats—which has built more America's Cup

boats than anyone else in the world—may just determine where the trophy resides after March 2000.

Boat speed is one thing, but how it is harnessed and used strategically and tactically during battle transfers the game from designers to sailors. Baird and his all-world crew know this as well as any of the challengers, and they have covered more than 3,000 miles in practice on Rhode Island Sound. They have also trained on the America's Cup course in Auckland.

On paper, this team looks to be an overwhelming favorite, but it is important to remember history. The New York Yacht Club's America II syndicate seemed made of the same ingredients in 1986 before they disintegrated in the waters Down Under. Have important lessons been learned? Will the America's Cup be returned to the yacht club that founded the trophy? Stay tuned.

The Young America team that trained in Auckland at the end of 1998 posed for a portrait aboard the yacht that competed in the '95 Cup match against Team New Zealand.

YEAR	WINNING YACHT	YACHT CLUB/NATION	SKIPPER	DESIGNER	SCORE
1851	America	New York Yacht Club/USA	C. Brown	George Steers	
1870	Magic	New York Yacht Club/USA	A.Comstock	R.S. Loper	1-0
1871	Columbia/ Sappho	New York Yacht Club/USA	N. Comstock/ S. Greenwood	J.VanDeusen/ D. Kerby	4-1
1876	Madeleine	New York Yacht Club/USA	J. Williams	G.A Smith	2-0
1881	Mischief	New York Yacht Club/USA	N. Clock	A. Cary Smith	2-0
1885	Puritan	New York Yacht Club/USA	A. J. Crocker	Edward Burgess	2-0
1886	Mayflower	New York Yacht Club/USA	M. Stone	Edward Burgess	2-0
1887	Volunteer	New York Yacht Club/USA	H. C. Haff	Edward Burgess	2-0
1893	Vigilant	New York Yacht Club/USA	W. Hansen	N. Herreshoff	3-0
1895	Defender	New York Yacht Club/USA	H. C. Haff	N. Herreshoff	3-0
1899	Columbia	New York Yacht Club/USA	C. Barr	N. Herreshoff	3-0
1901	Columbia	New York Yacht Club/USA	C.Barr	N. Herreshoff	3-0
1903	Reliance	New York Yacht Club/USA	C. Barr	N. Herreshoff	3-0
1920	Resolute	New York Yacht Club/USA	C. F. Adams	N. Herreshoff	3-2
1930	Enterprise	New York Yacht Club/USA	H. Vanderbilt	Starling Burgess	4-0
1934	Rainbow	New York Yacht Club/USA	H. Vanderbilt	Starling Burgess	4-2
1937	Ranger	New York Yacht Club/USA	H. Vanderbilt	S.Burgess/O. Stephens	4-0
1958	Columbia	New York Yacht Club/USA	B. Cunningham	Olin Stephens	4-0
1962	Weatherly	New York Yacht Club/USA	B. Mosbacher	Phil Rhodes	4-1
1964	Constellation	New York Yacht Club/USA	R. Bavier/E. Ridder	Olin Stephens	4-0
1967	Intrepid	New York Yacht Club/USA	B. Mosbacher	Olin Stephens	4-0
1970	Intrepid	New York Yacht Club/USA	B. Ficker	O.Stephens/B. Chance	4-1
1974	Courageous	New York Yacht Club/USA	R. Bavier	Olin Stephens	4-0
1977	Courageous	New York Yacht Club/USA	T. Turner	Sparkman & Stephens	4-0
1980	Freedom	New York Yacht Club/USA	D. Conner	Sparkman & Stephens	4-1
1983	Australia II	Royal Perth Yacht Club/Australia	J. Bertrand	Ben Lexcen	4-0
1987	Stars & Stripes	San Diego Yacht Club/USA	D. Conner	Design Team	4-0
1988	Stars & Stripes	San Diego Yacht Club/USA	D. Conner	Design Team	3-0
1992	America3	San Diego Yacht Club/USA	B. Koch	Design Team	4-1
1995	Black Magic	Royal NZ Yacht Squadron/New Zealand	Russell Coutts	Design Team	5-0

LOCATION	RIVAL YACHT	YACHT CLUB/NATION	SKIPPER	DESIGNER
Cowes, GB	Fleet of 15 British yachts			
New York, USA	Cambria	Royal Thames/Great Britain	J. Tannock	M. Ratsey
New York, USA	Livonia	Royal HarwichGreat Britain	J.R. Woods	M. Ratsey
New York, USA	Countess of Dufferin	Royal Canadian/Canada	J.E. Ellsworth	A.Cuthbert
New York, USA	Atalanta	Bay of Quinte/Canada	J.E. Ellsworth	A.Cuthbert
New York, USA	Genesta	Royal Yacht Squadron/Great Britain	J. Carter	J. Beavor-Webb
New York, USA	Galatea	Royal Northern/Great Britain	J. Carter	J. Beavor-Webb
New York, USA	Thistle	Royal Clyde/Great Britain	J. Barr	George Watson
New York, USA	Valkyrie II	Royal Yacht Squadron/Great Britain	W. Cranfield	George Watson
New York, USA	Valkyrie III	Royal Yacht Squadron/Great Britain	W. Cranfield	George Watson
New York, USA	Shamrock I	Royal Ulster/Northern Ireland	A. Hogarth	William Fife Jr.
New York, USA	Shamrock I	Royal Ulster/Northern Ireland	E. A. Sycamore	George Watson
New York, USA	Shamrock I	Royal Ulster/Northern Ireland	R. Wringe	William Fife Jr.
New York, USA	Shamrock I	Royal Ulster/Northern Ireland	W. Burton	Charles E. Nicholson
Newport, USA	Shamrock I	Royal Ulster/Northern Ireland	N. Heard	Charles E. Nicholson
Newport, USA	Endeavour	Royal Yacht Squadron/Great Britain	T.O.M. Sopwith	Charles E. Nicholson
Newport, USA	Endeavour	Royal Yacht Squadron/Great Britain	T.O.M. Sopwith	Charles E. Nicholson
Newport, USA	Sceptre	Royal Yacht Squadron/Great Britain	G. Mann	David Boyd
Newport, USA	Gretel	Royal Sydney Yacht Squadron/Australia	J. Sturrock	Alan Payne
Newport, USA	Sovereign	Royal Thames/Great Britain	P. Scott	David Boyd
Newport, USA	Dame Pattie	Royal Sydney Yacht Squadron/Australia	J. Sturrock	Warwick Hood
Newport, USA	Gretel II	Royal Sydney Yacht Squadron/Australia	J. Hardy	Alan Payne
Newport, USA	Souther Cross	Royal Perth Yacht Club/Australia	J. Cuneo	Bob Miller (Ben Lexcen)
Newport, USA	Australia	Sun City/Australia	N. Robins	Ben Lexcen/Johan Valentijn
Newport, USA	Australia	Royal Perth Yacht Club/Australia	J. Hardy	Ben Lexcen/Johan Valentijn
Perth, Australia	Liberty	New York Yacht Club/USA	D. Conner	Johan Valentijn
San Diego, USA	Kookaburra III	Royal Perth Yacht Club/Australia	I. Murray	Design Team led by Murray
San Diego, USA	New Zealand	Mercury Bay Boating Club/New Zealand	D. Barnes	Design Team led by B. Farr
San Diego, USA	Il Moro di Venezia	Compagnia della Vela/Italy	P. Cayard	Design Team
San Diego, USA	Young America	New York Yacht Club/USA	D. Conner	Design Team

INDEX

100 Guineas Cup 11, 15, 73, 91

6th sens **145**

A

Abracadabra 2000 159, 161

Advance 154

America 12, 15, 16, 73, 91

America ³ 50, **51**, **53**, 54, **65**, 79, 80, **83**, 85, **95**, 115, 128, 131, 160, 165, 171, 172, 177, 179

American Mischief 19

AmericaOne 162, **163**, 165, 166

America's Cup, The

  1876 19

  1881 19

  1882 19

  1886 19

  1887 19

  1903 75

  1920 16

  1930 25

  1934 20, 26, 29

  1937 20

  1958 29

  1962 25, 29

  1967 26

  1974 29, 31

  1977 30

  1987 44, 45, 122, 153

  1992 82, 87

  1995 91, 93, 128

  2000 111, 115, 122, 127, 128, 175, 184

America True 168, 169

Andrews, Dr. Jim 159, **161**

Anglesey, Marquis of 15

Appleton, Cameron 122

Argo, Stu 182

Ashbury, John 15, 16

Atlanta 19

Aurora 15

Australia **30**, 153

Australia II 26, 32, 35, **37**, **38**, 47, 76, **80**, 108, 115, 160

Australia III 46

Australia IV 47

B

Baird, Ed **182**, 184

Baker, Dean 120, 122

Baylis, Liz 171

Beer, Ben 171

Belsky, Josh 165

Bertelli, Patrizio 131, **133**, **134**

Bertrand, John 32, 35, **39**, 52, 61, 63, 153

Bich, Baron Marcel 31, 32, 144

Blackaller, Tom 35, 159

Black Magic 52, 57, 79, **92**, 108, 115, 117, 122, 127, **129**

Blake, Peter 117, 121, 128

Blewett, Curtis 165

Bond, Alan 31, 32, **39**, 47

Brady, Jim **184**

Briand, Philippe 148, **150**

Burgess, Edward 19, 23,

Burgess, W.S. 26

Burnham, Tom 182

Burns, Ian 160

C

Calder, Steve 182

Cambell, Bill 182

Cambria 16, 91

Campos, Pedro 141, **142**, 143

Carrey, Merritt 171

Cavalazzi, Guido 133

Cayard, Paul 50, 94, 162, 165, **166**

Challenge Australia 154

Chance, Britton 76

Chieffi, Enrico 148

Chirac, Jacques 146

Ciparik, Judge Carmen Beauchamp 49

Clark, James H. 162

Clarkson, Sean 165

Clipper 32

Coello, Joaquin 143

Coffin, G. Christopher 169, 171

Columbia **14**, **22**, 23, 29

Conner, Dennis **28**, 32, 35, 36, 38, **44**, 47, 49, 50, 52, 54, 57, 63, 65, 76, 80, 106, 119, 123, 128, 136, 144, 153, 156, 159, 160, 162, 165, **174**, 175, **178**

Constellation **24**, 25, 29

Constitution 75

Cortez Racing Association 128

Courageous 23, **28**, **30**, 31, 32, 76, 159, 177

Coutts, Russell 52, **57**, **117**, 119, 120, 121, 122, 172

Cunningham, Briggs **23**

Cuthbert, Alexander 19

Cutler, John 136, **170**

D

Dagg, James **122**

Dame Pattie 26, 31, 153

Daubney, Simon **118**, 122

Davidson, Laurie **123**, 131

Davis, Rod 50, 135

de Angelis, Francesco 133, **134**, 135

Defender 20, 76, 135, 159

Dickson, Chris 46, 91, 106, 121, 128, 136, 182

Doreste, Luis **142**, 143

Dovell, Andy 160

Drummond, Mike 119, 120

E

Eagle 135

Earl of Dunraven 20

EF Language 165

Egan, David 119, 133

Egnot, Leslie **170**, 171, **172**

Endeavour 20, 26

Endeavour II 20, 26

Enterprise 23, 25, 32, 76, **78**, **79**, 135

Erickson, Steve 164

España 95 141

Esquier, Laurent 135

F

Fachler, Marcel 43, 44

Farr, Bruce 143, 182, **184**

Fay, Michael 43, 44, 49, 182

Fischer, Syd **154**, 156

France II 144

France 3 144, 147

Freedom 32, **34**, 144, 177

Freedom '83 159

French Kiss 146, 148, 160

Frers, German 131

Frers, German Jr. 133

G

Galatea 19

Gale, Jamie 182

Gardini, Raul 50, 82

Gelluseau, Luc 146, **147**

Genesta 19

Gilmour, Peter 136, **138**, 139

Grael, Torben 135

Gretel **24**, 29, 75, 153

Gretel II 31, 144, 153, 156

H

Halcrow, Ross 182

Hardy, James 156

Herreshoff, Nathanael **12**, 16, 20, 23, 32, 75

Holmberg, Peter 177, **179**
Holroyd, Nick 119
Hood, Ted 32
Hutchinson, Terry 165

I
Il Moro di Venezia 49, 50, **53**, **65**, 79, **83**, **95**, 131, 135, 141, 160
Independence 32
Intrepid 23, **26**, 31, 76, 79, 180

J
Jewett, George "Fritz" Jr. 162
Jobson, Gary 32, 35, 159
Jones, Murray **120**, 122
Jones, Warren 153
Jordan, Hartwell 182

K
Kaiko, Phil 172
Kiwi Magic 43, 47
Koch, Bill 50, 52, **54**, 79, 82, 128, 131, 172, 177, 184
Kolius, John 35, 159, 160, 161
Kookaburra III 44, 47, 49, 79, 106, **153**
Kostecki, John 165

L
Lexcen, Ben 32, **36**, 153

Liberty 32, 35, **37**, **38**, 76, 159, 160, 177
Lipton, Sir Thomas 15, 16, 20, 23, 26, 75, 79, 154
Livonia 16, 91
Long, Russell 32
Loretz, Grant 120, 121
Louis Vuitton Cup 50, 57, 117, 121, 123, 131, 136, 138, 139, 166
Luna Rossa **130**, 133

M
MacBeth, John 120
MacKay, Barry 120, 121
MacLane, Duncan 180
Madeline 19
Magic 16
Mariner 76, **77**, 177
Marshall, John 128, 180, 182
Mayflower 19
Melges, Buddy 94, **172**, 179
Mighty Mary 108, 172
Milgram, Dr. Jerry 184
Mitchell, Matthew 122
Miyata, Hideaki 139
Monk, Craig **118**
Morgan, J. Pierpont 20
Mosbacher, Bus 29
Murray, Iain 47

N
Namba, Makoto 136, 138
Nelson, Bruce 162, **166**
New Zealand 135
Nippon Challenge 50, **90**, 120, 136, 138, 139, 141, 171
North, Lowell 32
Nyala 131

O
Oliver, Clay 119
oneAustralia 52, 135, 154, **157**, 160, 177

P
Pacé, Bertrand 146, **147**
Packard, Sir Frank 31
Paine, Charles J. 19
Pajot, Marc 144, 146, 147, 148, **151**
Parry, Kevin 47
Paulu de la Barriere, Philippe 147
Payne, Alan 29, 76, 153
Pepper, Hamish 122
Peterson, Doug 119, 131
Pettibone, Katie 171, **173**
Phipps, Dean **118**, 122
Pillot, Luc 146
Prada, Miuccia 131, **132**
Pugh, Jim 179
Puritan 19

R

Rainbow **21**, 26
Ranger **18**, **21**, 26, 32
Read, Ken 177
Reichel, John 177
Reliance 23, **74**, 75, 76
Resolute **17**, 23
Rey, Tony 182
Rice, Bob 120
Riley, Dawn 169, **170**, **171**
Rioja de España **140**, 141
Rockefeller, William 20

S

Sceptre 23, 29
Schnackenberg, Tom 119
Schumann, Jochen 148, **151**
Schuyler, George 15, 19
Sears, Harry **23**
Sefton, Alan 117
Shamrock II **14**, 16, 75
Shamrock IV 20, 23, 26
Shamrock V 23, 25, 79
Sopwith, T.O.M. 26, 29
Southern Cross 29, 31, 76, 144, 153
Sovereign **25**
Spanhake, Mike 136, 182
Sparkman, Drake 19, 26
Spirit of Australia 161

Spithill, James 154, 156
Stars and Stripes **42**, 44, 52, 54, 57, **62**, 65, 76, 80, 106, 119, 153, 165, 179, 180
Stephens, Olin 19, **23**, 26, 29, 32, 35, 76, 131
Stephens, Rod 19, 26
Stevens, John Cox 12, 15
Sydney 95 155, 156
Sydney Steak 'n' Kidney 156

T

Tag Heuer 121, 128, 182
Thistle 20
Trenkle, Bill **176**, 177
Troublé, Bruno 144
Turner, Ted 32, **33**, 35, 177
Tutukaka Challenge 136

V

Valentine, Johann 35
Valkyrie II 12, 20
Valkyrie III 20
Vanderbilt, Cornelius 20
Vanderbilt, Harold **19**, 23, 29
Victory 35
Vigilant 13, 20
Volunteer 19
Vrolijk, Rolf 143

W

Ward, Chris **121**
Weatherly 29, 153
Williams, Erle 136
Worthington, Kimo 165, 182

Y

Yamaski, Tatsumitsu 136, 139
Young America 52, 54, **92**, 127, **129**, 131, 162, 166, 180, 182, 184, **185**
Young Australia 2000 154, 156

PHOTO CREDITS